CB078503

Pathway to Math 1

Student's Book

Glue your picture here.

Name

Richmond

Richmond
58 St Aldates
Oxford
OX1 1ST
United Kingdom

Pathway to Math Student's Book Level 1

First Edition: January 2016
First Reprint: March 2017
ISBN: 978-607-06-1255-8

Pathway to Math 1 is a collaborative work, created and designed by the Department of Educational Research of Santillana. Richmond adapted the project and created an English version.
© Ángela Baeza Peña, Fátima López Vergara, María Paulina Sandoval Labarca, Andrea Urra
© Richmond Publishing, S.A. de C.V. 2016
Av. Río Mixcoac No. 274, Col. Acacias,
Benito Juárez, C.P. 03240, Ciudad de México

Publisher: Justine Piekarowicz
Editorial Team: Matthew Bifano, Natalia Herrera, Duncan Jones, Jacaranda Ruiz
Pre-Press Coordinator: Daniel Santillán
Cover Design: Lourdes Arroyo

Cover Photograph: ©THINKSTOCK: iStock (Dejan_Dundjerski)

Illustrations: Paula Gutiérrez Fischman, Ma José González Margossini

Photographs: Archivo Santillana
©THINKSTOCK: iStock pp. 19, 31, 45, 63, 81, 97, 115, 135, 151 (graphic-bee), 19, 31, 45, 63, 81, 97, 115, 135, 151 (luctra_design), 64,85 (tassel78).

All rights reserved. No part of this work may be reproduced, stored in a retrieval system or transmitted in any form or by any means without prior written permission from the Publisher.

Richmond publications may contain links to third party websites or apps. We have no control over the content of these websites or apps, which may change frequently, and we are not responsible for the content or the way it may be used with our materials. Teachers and students are advised to exercise discretion when accessing the links.

The Publisher has made every effort to trace the owner of copyrighted material; however, the Publisher will correct any involuntary omission at the earliest opportunity.

Printed in Brazil by Forma Certa Gráfica Digital
Lote: 808131
Codigo: 292712558 / 2025

Introduction

Hi friends!

We are **Spot**  and **Kiki**  and we are here to welcome you to **Pathway to Math**. Follow us on the Pathway to Math, where learning becomes special. Do you want to know why?

- This pathway is full of magic, and everyone is welcome on it. You will find information, texts, pictures and activities presented in a simple and friendly manner. Here you will discover that learning is fun!
- This is a pathway where we can all learn to share and live together. The activities will help us reflect on our values and learn to respect others.

- This is a pathway open to people from all over the world where you can learn interactively with the help of the latest technology.
- This is a pathway full of challenges that involve finding solutions, developing math skills and applying calculation strategies that you and your classmates will work on together.

We will be with you every step of the way!
All you need is curiosity and the desire to learn.

How is your textbook organized?

Pathway to Math 1 is organized into five units. Here is what you will find in each unit.

Initial Pages

- Number and title of the unit
- Learning objectives
- Initial evaluation

Sections Organized by Learning Objectives

- Let's Connect
  Observe and answer.
- Let's Learn
- Let's Practice
- Quiz Yourself

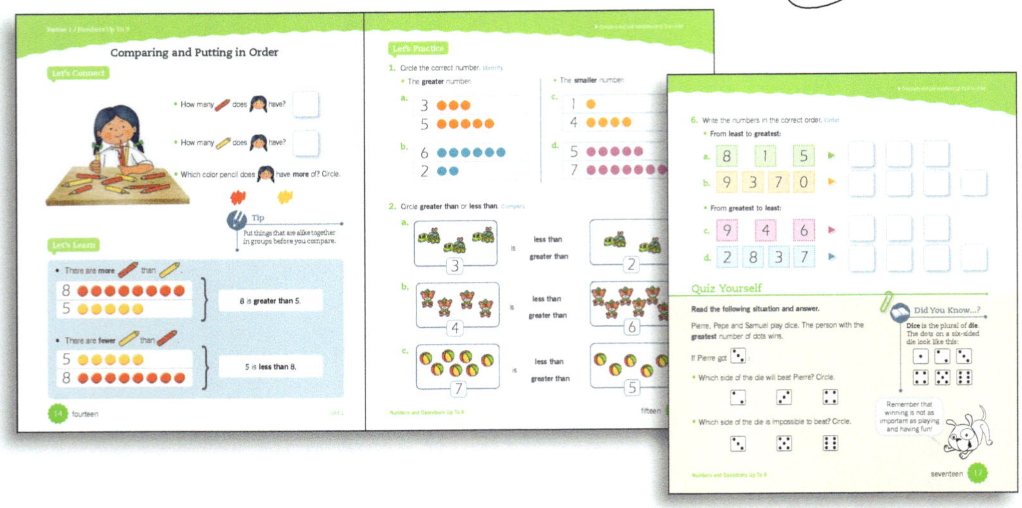

Fun Features

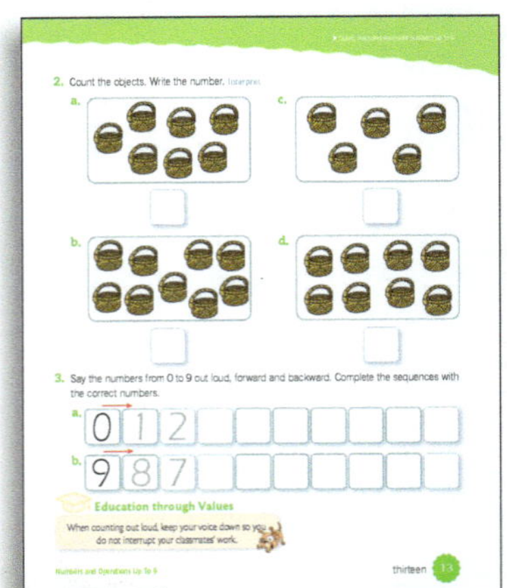

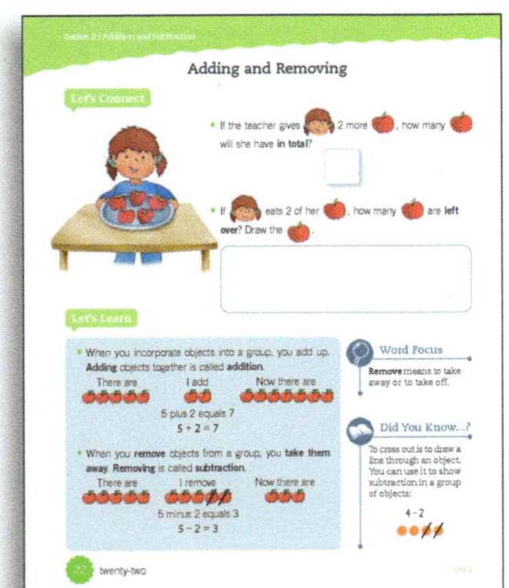

- Education through Values
- Did You Know...?
- Remember
- Tip
- Word Focus
- Fun Fact!
- Challenge

Evaluation Pages

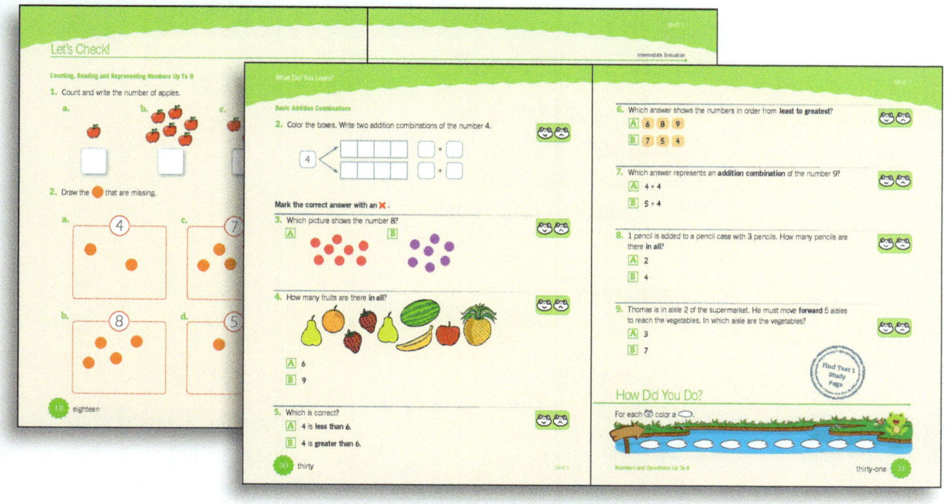

- What Do You Know?
  Initial Evaluation
- Let's Check!
  Intermediate Evaluation
- What Did You Learn?
  Final Evaluation

Special Pages

- Exam Strategies
- Test Study Pages
  Summary and Review

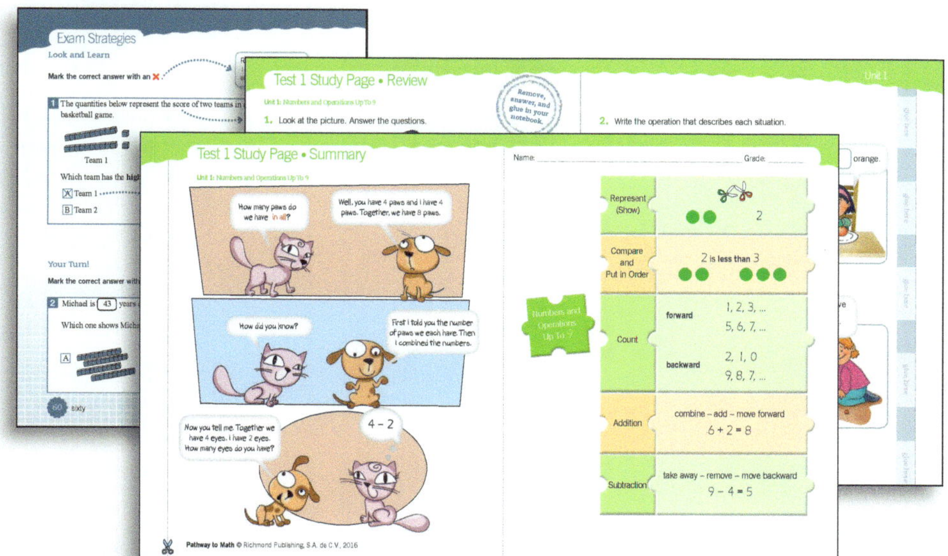

Support Pages

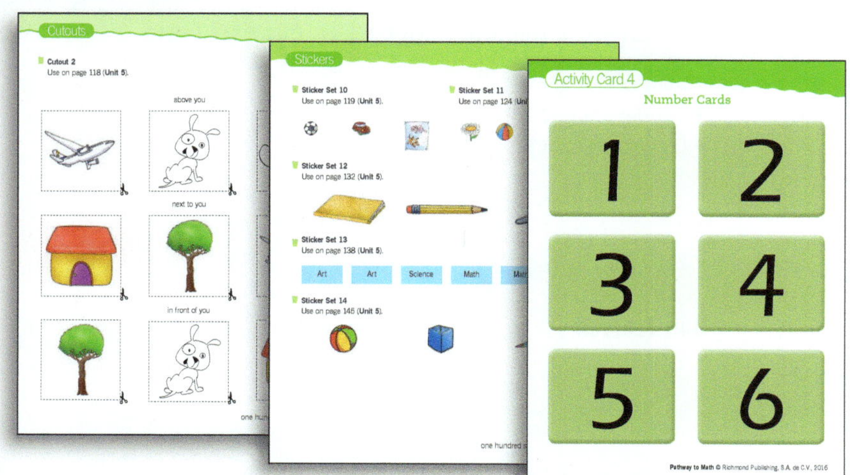

- Cutouts
- Stickers
- Activity Cards

Table of Contents

Unit 1

Numbers and Operations Up To 9

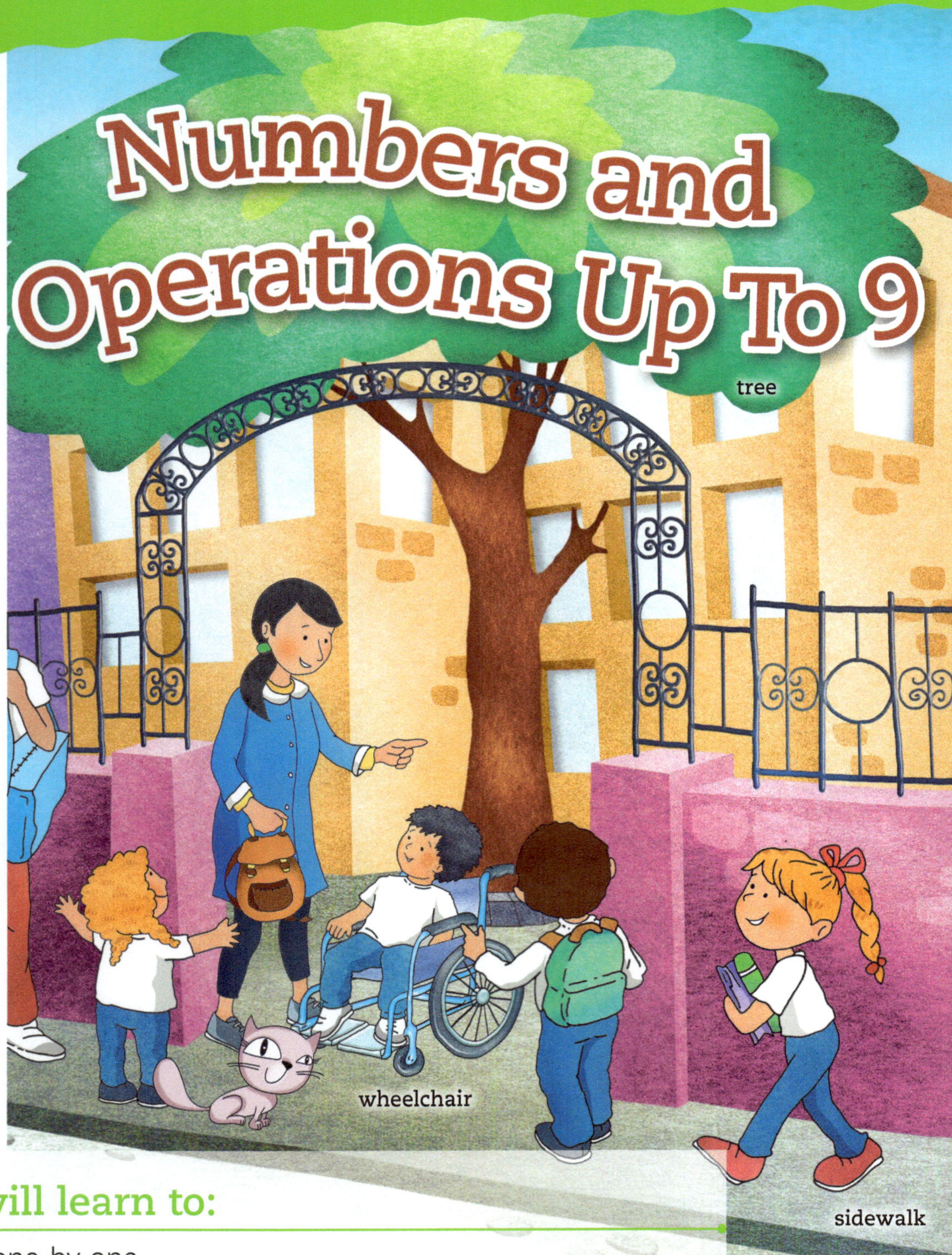

Key Words

count

order

combine

add

subtract

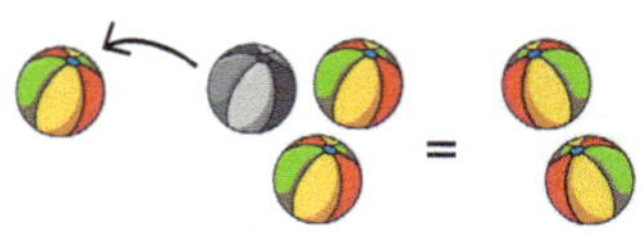

In this unit you will learn to:

- count up to number 9 one by one.
- read and write numbers up to 9 using pictures and symbols.
- compare and organize numbers up to 9.
- represent addition and subtraction using combine and take away, add and remove and move forward and backward.
- use basic addition combinations.
- show curiosity and interest in learning math.
- do your work in a clear and organized way.

What Do You Know?

Initial Evaluation

Look at the picture. Discuss with your class.

1. How many boys and girls are there in the picture? Show the amount using **Sticker Set 1** on **page 169**.

2. How many adults are there? Circle.

1 3 5

3. Circle the group that has **more**  .

Numbers Up To 9

Counting, Reading and Representing

Let's Connect

Circle your answers.

- How many 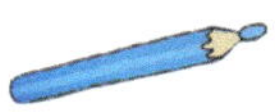 does  have?

4 5 6

- How many  does  have?

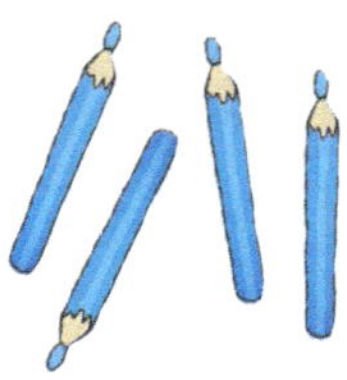 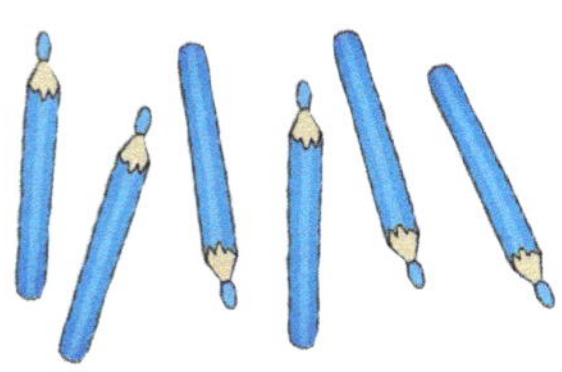 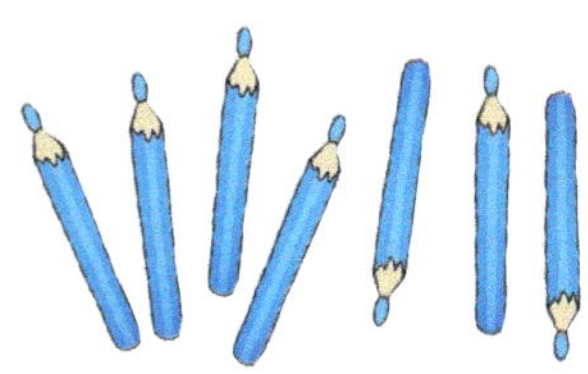

- Which group of  represents the number of 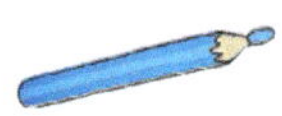 that  has?

 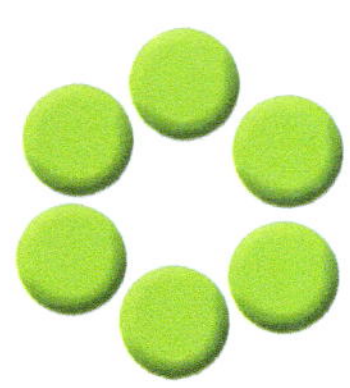 

Let's Learn

0
zero

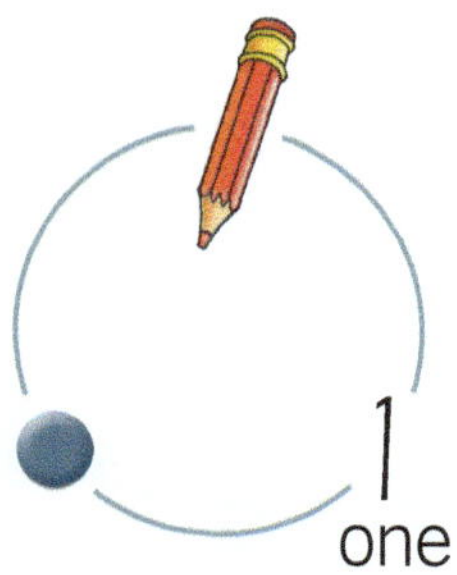

1
one

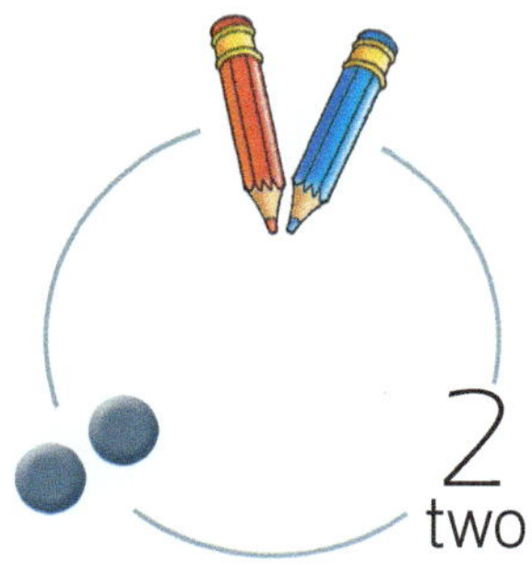

2
two

3
three

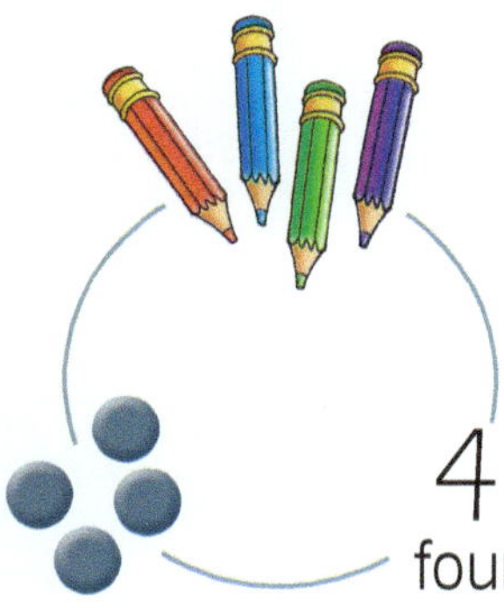

4
four

5
five

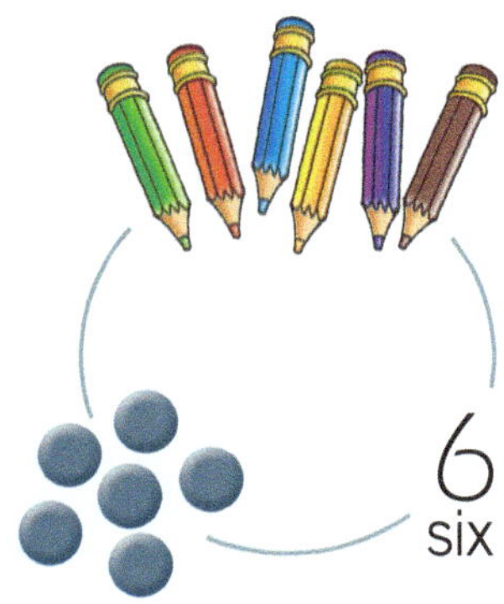

6
six

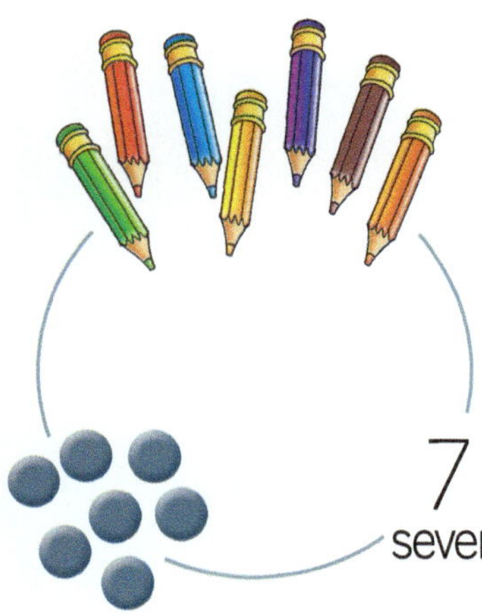

7
seven

8
eight

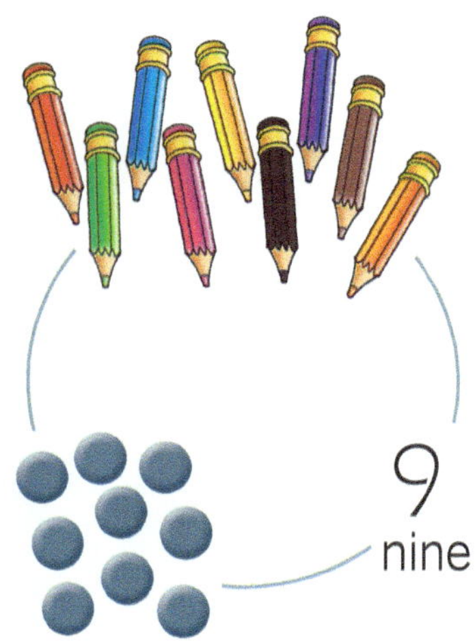

9
nine

Let's Practice

1. Count the number of animals in each group. Match them with the correct number. Relate

2. Count the objects. Write the number. Interpret

a.

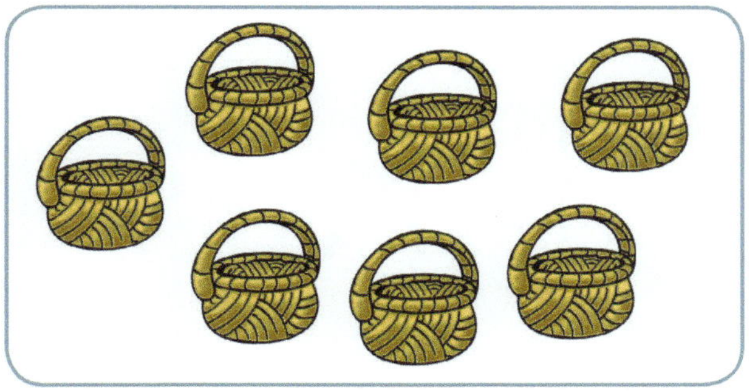

c.

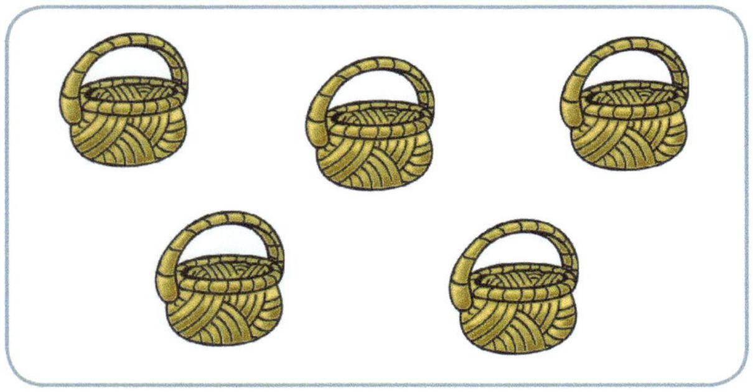

b.

d.

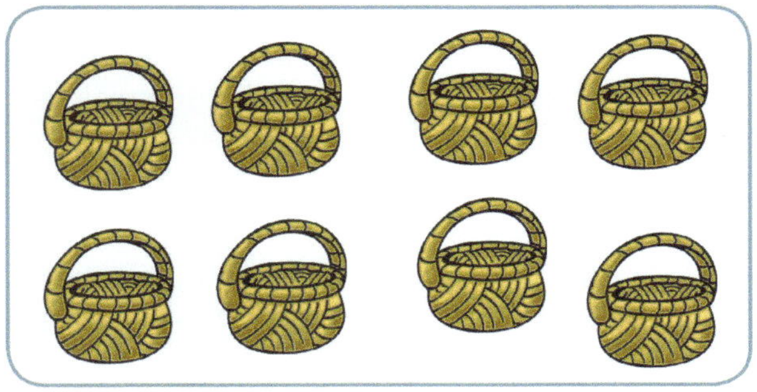

3. Say the numbers from 0 to 9 out loud, forward and backward. Complete the sequences with the correct numbers.

a. 0 1 2

b. 9 8 7

Education through Values

When counting out loud, keep your voice down so you do not interrupt your classmates' work.

Comparing and Putting in Order

Let's Connect

- How many does have?
- How many does have?
- Which color pencil does have **more** of? Circle.

Tip

Put things that are alike together in groups before you compare.

Let's Learn

- There are **more** than .

8

5

8 is **greater than** 5.

- There are **fewer** than .

5

8

5 is **less than** 8.

Let's Practice

1. Circle the correct number. Identify

- The **greater** number:

a.

3 

5 

b.

6 

2 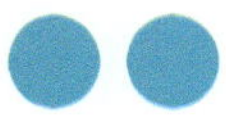

- The **smaller** number:

c.

1 

4 

d.

5 

7 

2. Circle **greater than** or **less than**. Compare

a.

3 is **less than** / **greater than**

2

b.

4 is **less than** / **greater than**

6

c.

7 is **less than** / **greater than**

5

3. Color each number with the correct color. Compare

the **smallest** number — the **greatest** number

a.	0	1	2	**c.**	7	9	5	**e.**	8	6	4
b.	5	7	8	**d.**	2	4	3	**f.**	1	6	9

4. Choose and write a number. Apply

- **Greater than**:

a. 3 ☐ **b.** 6 ☐ **c.** 8 ☐

- **Less than**:

d. ☐ 1 **e.** ☐ 9 **f.** ☐ 5

5. Write a number that is **less than** or **greater than** the number given. Apply

a. ☐ 2 ☐ **c.** ☐ 6 ☐

b. ☐ 4 ☐ **d.** ☐ 7 ☐

6. Write the numbers in the correct order. Order

- From **least** to **greatest:**

a. 8 1 5 ▶

b. 9 3 7 0 ▶

- From **greatest** to **least:**

c. 9 4 6 ▶

d. 2 8 3 7 ▶

Quiz Yourself

Read the following situation and answer.

Pierre, Pepe and Samuel play dice. The person with the **greatest** number of dots wins.

If Pierre got  :

- Which side of the die will beat Pierre? Circle.

- Which side of the die is impossible to beat? Circle.

Did You Know...?

Dice is the plural of **die**. The dots on a six-sided die look like this:

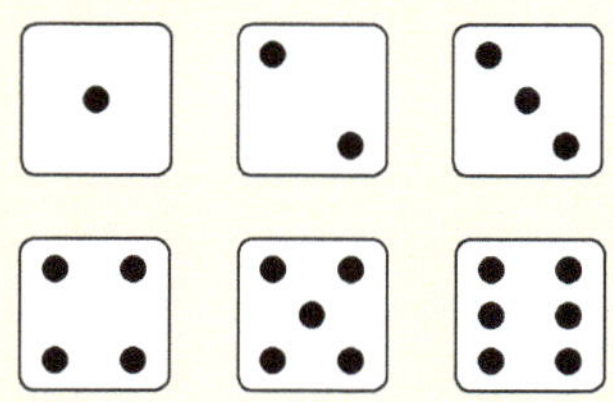

Remember that winning is not as important as playing and having fun!

Let's Check!

Counting, Reading and Representing Numbers Up To 9

1. Count and write the number of apples.

a.

b.

c.

2. Draw the ● that are missing.

a. 4

c. 7

b. 8

d. 5

Comparing and Putting Numbers Up To 9 in Order

3. Circle the group that has **more** socks.

a.

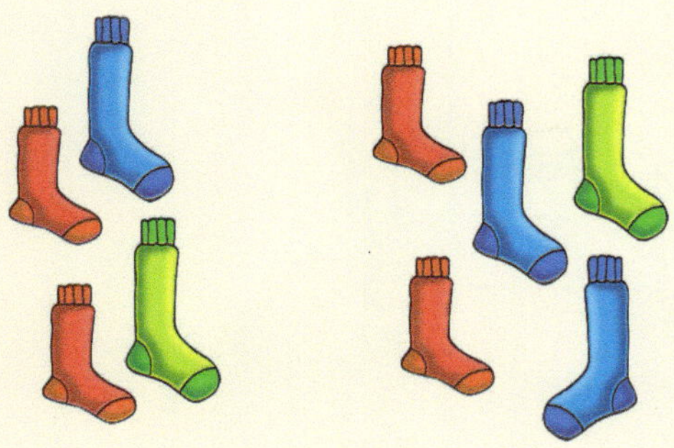

b.

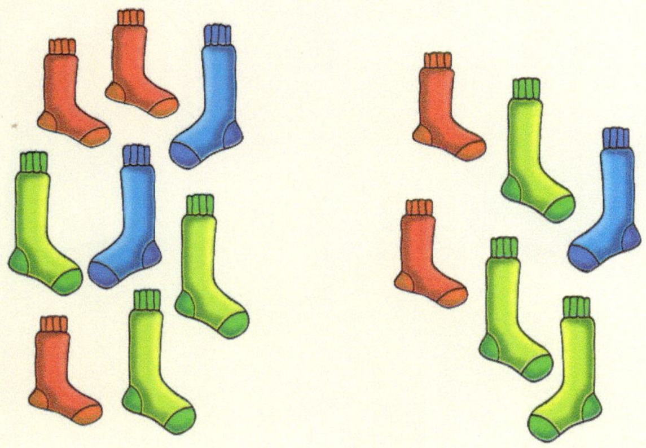

4. Circle **greater than** or **less than** for each.

a. 2 is **less than** / **greater than** 0

b. 5 is **less than** / **greater than** 8

c. 1 is **less than** / **greater than** 7

d. 9 is **less than** / **greater than** 3

How Did You Do?

For each color a .

Section 2
Addition and Subtraction

Combining and Taking Away

Let's Connect

- How many blocks does each tower have?

 ☐  ☐

- If the children **combine** their blocks and build one tower, how many blocks will the new tower have?

☐

- If  **takes away** his blocks from the new tower, how many blocks will be left? Show the amount with ●.

Let's Learn

- **Combining** is related to **addition**.

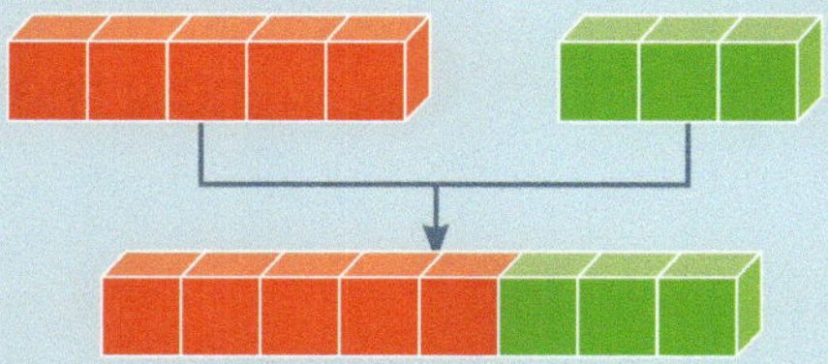

5 plus 3 equals 8 — 3 plus 5 equals 8

$5 + 3 = 8$ — $3 + 5 = 8$

- **Taking away** is related to **subtraction**.

8 minus 3 equals 5 — 8 minus 5 equals 3

$8 - 3 = 5$ — $8 - 5 = 3$

Let's Practice

1. Count, combine and complete. Apply

a.

☐ plus ☐ equals ☐

☐ ☐ ☐ = ☐

b.

☐ plus ☐ equals ☐

☐ ☐ ☐ = ☐

2. Read, take away and complete. Apply

a. Out of 8 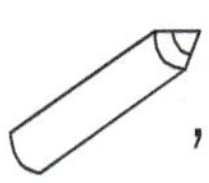, 5 are orange and the rest are blue. How many are blue?

☐ minus ☐ equals ☐

☐ ☐ ☐ = ☐

b. Out of 9 , 3 are yellow and the rest are green. How many are green?

☐ minus ☐ equals ☐

☐ ☐ ☐ = ☐

Adding and Removing

Let's Connect

- If the teacher gives 2 more , how many will she have **in total**?

- If eats 2 of her , how many are **left over**? Draw the .

Let's Learn

- When you incorporate objects into a group, you add up. **Adding** objects together is called **addition**.

There are . I add . Now there are .

5 plus 2 equals 7

$5 + 2 = 7$

- When you **remove** objects from a group, you **take them away**. **Removing** is called **subtraction**.

There are . I remove . Now there are .

5 minus 2 equals 3

$5 - 2 = 3$

Word Focus

Remove means to take away or to take off.

Did You Know...?

To cross out is to draw a line through an object. You can use it to show subtraction in a group of objects:

$4 - 2$

Let's Practice

1. Look at each picture. Complete. Apply

a.

There are ☐ .　☐ arrive.　Now there are ☐ .

☐ ☐ ☐ = ☐

b.

There are ☐ .　☐ leave.　Now there are ☐ .

☐ ☐ ☐ = ☐

2. Draw pictures to add. Cross out pictures to remove. Complete. Apply

a. Dan has 6 balls.
He gives 2 to Amy.
How many balls does
he have left?

☐ ☐ ☐ = ☐

b. Sally has 5 flowers.
Her family gives her 1 more.
How many flowers does
she have now?

☐ ☐ ☐ = ☐

Challenge

Sing and dance to "10 Little Monkeys." Ask your teacher for the song and lyrics. Perform it for the class with your friends.

Forward and Backward

Let's Connect

- Which square is each **token** on? Write the number.

 ☐  ☐

- How many squares should  move **forward** to reach  ?

☐

- How many squares should  move **backward** to reach  ?

☐

Let's Learn

- To move **forward**, you **add**. Moving **forward** is related to **addition**.

0	1	2	3	4	5	6	7	8	9

$2 + 5 = 7$

- To move **backward**, you **subtract**. Moving **backward** is related to **subtraction**.

0	1	2	3	4	5	6	7	8	9

$7 - 5 = 2$

Let's Practice

1. Go to **Cutout 1** on **page 159**. Use the numbered tape to count **forward** or **backward**. Complete.
Apply

0	1	2	3	4	5	6	7	8	9

a. I am on 3 → I move **forward** 1 → I reach ☐

b. I am on 6 → I move **backward** 2 → I reach ☐

c. I am on 4 → I move **forward** 5 → I reach ☐

Word Focus

Backward is the opposite of **forward**.

2. Write the math operation for each action below. Interpret

a.

0	1	2	3	4	5	6	7	8	9

☐ ☐ ☐ = ☐

b.

0	1	2	3	4	5	6	7	8	9

☐ ☐ ☐ = ☐

c.

0	1	2	3	4	5	6	7	8	9

☐ ☐ ☐ = ☐

Basic Addition Combinations

Let's Connect

- How many pencils of **each** color does each girl have?

and

and

and

- How many pencils does each girl have **in all**?

Let's Learn

Basic addition combinations are different ways of making the same number.

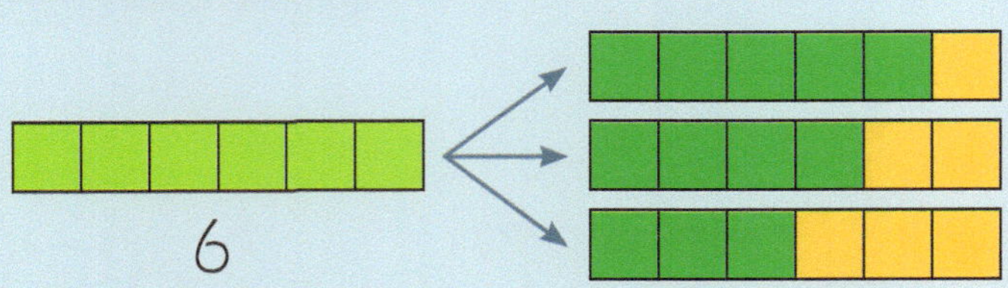

$5 + 1 = 6$

$4 + 2 = 6$

$3 + 3 = 6$

Let's Practice

1. Color the ☐ and write three basic addition combinations for each number. Complete. Apply

a. 7

☐ + ☐

☐ + ☐

☐ + ☐

b. 8

☐ + ☐

☐ + ☐

☐ + ☐

c. 9

☐ + ☐

☐ + ☐

☐ + ☐

Quiz Yourself

Look at the operation and answer.

6 – 2 =

- Which picture **represents** the previous operation? Circle.

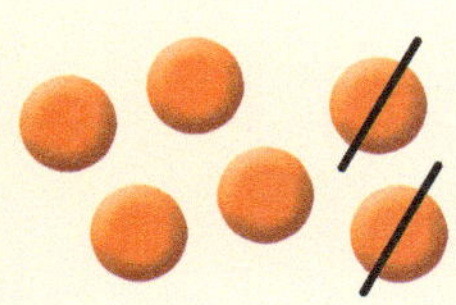

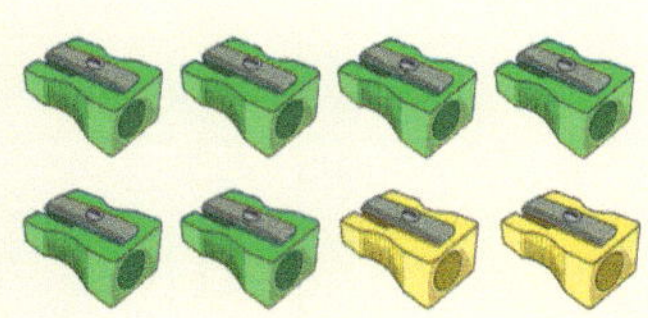

Exam Strategies

Look and Learn

Mark the correct answer with an ✗ .

Read the **instructions**. They will tell you how to answer the question.

1 Samuel has a box with 6 red tokens and 3 blue tokens. How many tokens does Samuel have **in all**?

A 3

~~B~~ 9

Read and understand the **question**. This is the question you must answer. Find a strategy that will help you answer this question.

These are the possible **answers**. One of them is the correct answer. Remember that you must choose one and mark it with an ✗.

Your Turn!

Mark the correct answer with an ✗ .

2 Amalia has 4 cookies and Pamela has 7 cookies. Who has more cookies?

A Amalia.

B Pamela.

What Did You Learn?

Final Evaluation

Daily Activities that Use Addition and Subtraction

1. Draw each situation. Write the operation.

a.

How many cards does [girl] have now?

☐ ☐ ☐ = ☐

b.

Which square do [girl] and [boy] reach?

☐ ☐ ☐ = ☐

c.

How many cars does [boy] have?

☐ ☐ ☐ = ☐

Basic Addition Combinations

2. Color the boxes. Write two addition combinations of the number 4.

Mark the correct answer with an ✕ .

3. Which picture shows the number 8?

A

B

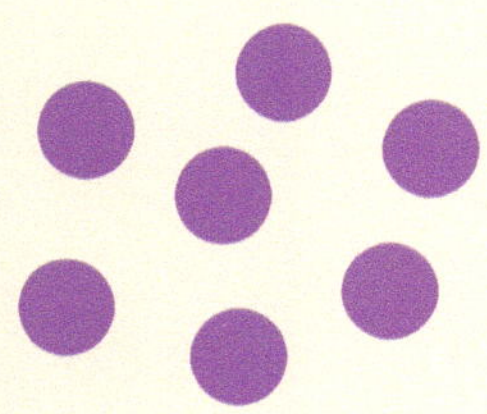

4. How many fruits are there **in all**?

A 6

B 9

5. Which is correct?

A 4 is **less than** 6.

B 4 is **greater than** 6.

6. Which answer shows the numbers in order from **least to greatest**?

A 6 8 9

B 7 5 4

7. Which answer represents an **addition combination** of the number 9?

A 4 + 4

B 5 + 4

8. 1 pencil is added to a pencil case with 3 pencils. How many pencils are there **in all**?

A 2

B 4

9. Thomas is in aisle 2 of the supermarket. He must move **forward** 5 aisles to reach the vegetables. In which aisle are the vegetables?

A 3

B 7

Find Test 1 Study Page

How Did You Do?

For each frog color a lily pad.

Numbers Up To 50

Key Words

ordinal numbers

cardinal numbers

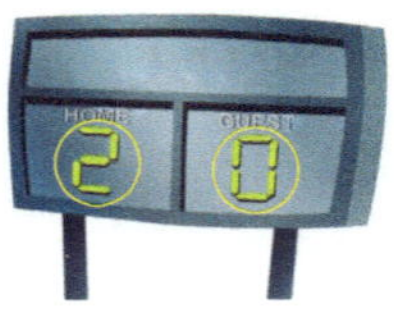

nominal numbers

represent

6 = 

In this unit you will learn to:

- count up to 50 one by one and count by grouping.
- represent numbers up to 50 using pictures and symbols.
- compare and put numbers up to 50 in order.
- identify different functions of numbers.
- recognize ones and tens in bigger numbers.
- use composition and decomposition in addition.
- do your work in a clear and organized way.

What Do You Know?

Initial Evaluation

Look at the picture and answer.

1. Draw 🔵 to represent the number of offspring each animal has.

Word Focus

Offspring means the young or babies of animals.

2. How many offspring does each animal have? Write the number.

3. Circle the animal with the **most** offspring.

Counting, Reading and Representing

Let's Connect

- How many  does  have? ☐
- How many  are on the table? Circle.

- Show the number of eggs on the table using **Sticker Set 2** on **page 169**.

Let's Learn

9 plus 1 equals 10 ten

10 plus 1

11 eleven

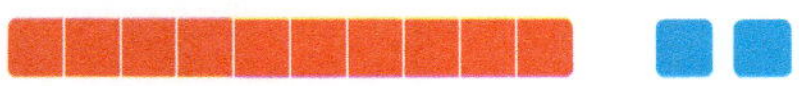

10 plus 2

12 twelve

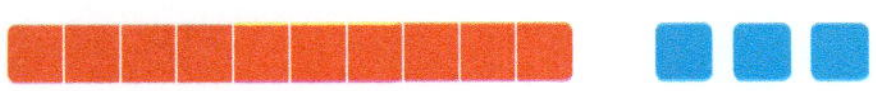

10 plus 3

13 thirteen

10 plus 4

14 fourteen

10 plus 5

15 fifteen

10 plus 6

16 sixteen

10 plus 7

17 seventeen

10 plus 8

18 eighteen

10 plus 9

19 nineteen

10 plus 10

20 twenty

Let's Practice

1. Count the fruit. Match them with the correct number. Relate

12

17

16

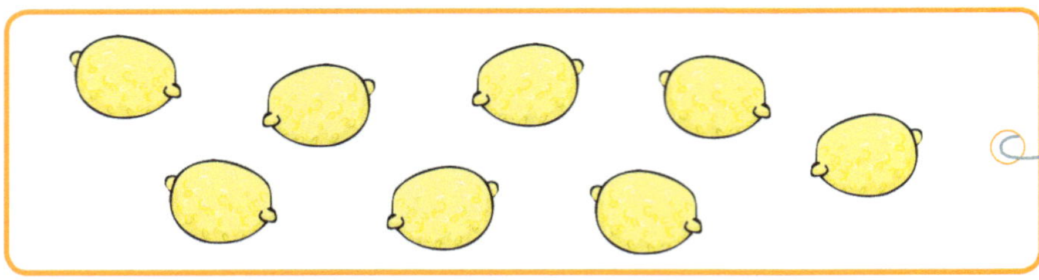

19

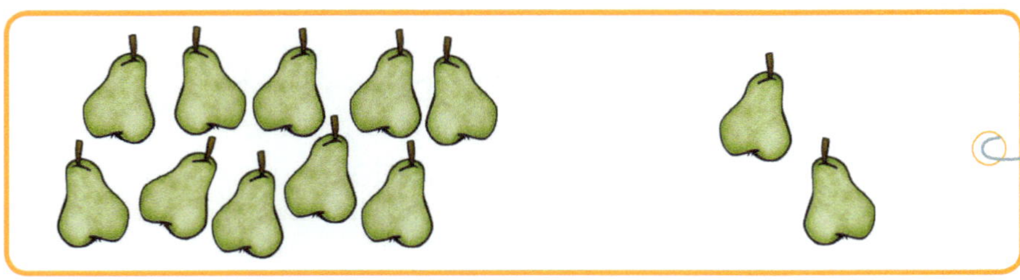

8

Education through Values

Fruit is yummy! It helps us grow and be healthy.

2. Represent each number. Use **Sticker Set 3** on **page 169**. Represent

a. 13

c. 16

b. 18

d. 15

3. Count the  . Write the correct number. Apply

a.

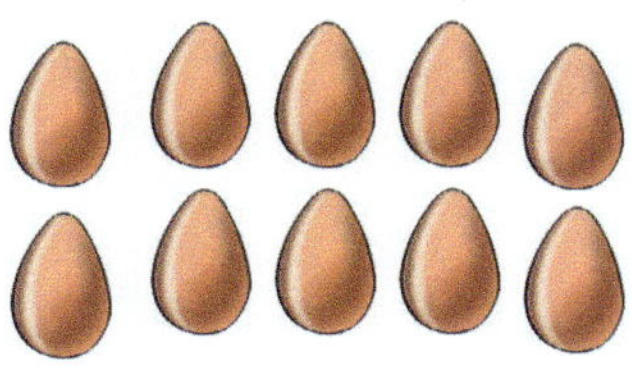

c.

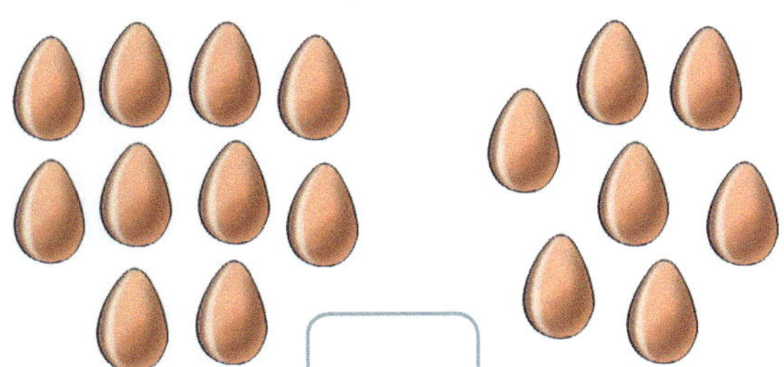

b.

d.

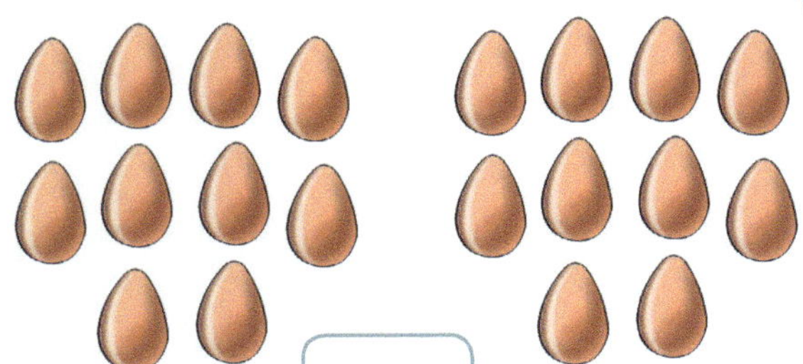

Comparing and Putting in Order

Let's Connect

- What would you do to put the cards in order from the **least** to the **greatest**? Color the ◯ with the correct answer.

◯ Combine the numbers. ◯ Count the numbers. ◯ Compare the numbers.

Let's Learn

To put numbers in **order** from the least to the greatest or from the greatest to the least, we **compare** them.

7 is **less than** 13, 7 is **less than** 10 → 7 is the **smallest** number.

10 is **less than** 13 → 13 is the **greatest** number.

So we can put the numbers in **order** from the **least** to the **greatest** like this:

7	10	13

Let's Practice

1. Circle **greater than** or **less than**. Compare

a. 12 is less than / greater than 6

b. 9 is less than / greater than 15

c. 1 is less than / greater than 10

d. 18 is less than / greater than 13

2. Put the numbers in order from the **greatest** to the **least**. Organize

a. 7 | 20 | 11 ▶ ☐ ☐ ☐

b. 14 | 17 | 10 ▶ ☐ ☐ ☐

Remember!

We learned in Unit 1 that **greatest** also means **biggest**.

Quiz Yourself

Use the hints to write the numbers in the correct boxes.

Hints:

- ■ (blue) is the greatest number.
- ■ (green) is greater than ■ (yellow).
- ■ (purple) is less than ■ (yellow).
- ■ (orange) is less than ■ (yellow) and ■ (purple).

20

14

16

10

Different Functions of Numbers

Ordinal Numbers

Let's Connect

- Circle the bicycle at the finish line.

- Put the bicycles in order. Use **Sticker Set 4** on **page 169**.

Let's Learn

1st first	2nd second	3rd third	4th fourth	5th fifth	6th sixth	7th seventh	8th eighth	9th ninth	10th tenth

These numbers indicate **order**, place or position. They are called **ordinal numbers**.

Let's Practice

Use the picture to answer the questions.

1. Write the **ordinal number** of the floor each person is on. Interpret

a.  ______

b.  ______

c.  ______

d.  ______

2. Go to **Sticker Set 5** on **page 169**. Place the objects according to the instructions. Apply

a. Put the curtains on the **sixth** floor.

b. Put the flowerpot on the **eighth** floor.

c. Put the bird on the **ninth** floor.

Challenge

Draw your own apartment building. Then draw a cat, a dog, a flower and yourself in different windows of the building. Do not show your picture to your partner. Now you and your partner will take turns asking questions to locate each item. For example, you can ask if the dog is on the third floor. The first person to locate all of their partner's items wins.

Nominal and Cardinal Numbers

Let's Connect

- Circle the **ordinal number** in the picture.
- Circle the boy wearing the shirt with the number 8.

- How many goals have been scored in the game?

Let's Learn

Numbers can be used to **order**, **identify** and **quantify**. They can function as ordinal, nominal and cardinal numbers.

order	identify	quantify
We use **ordinal numbers** to put things in order. 	Numbers can be used to identify people or objects. These numbers are called **nominal numbers.** 	Numbers can show a quantity or measurement. These numbers are called **cardinal numbers.** 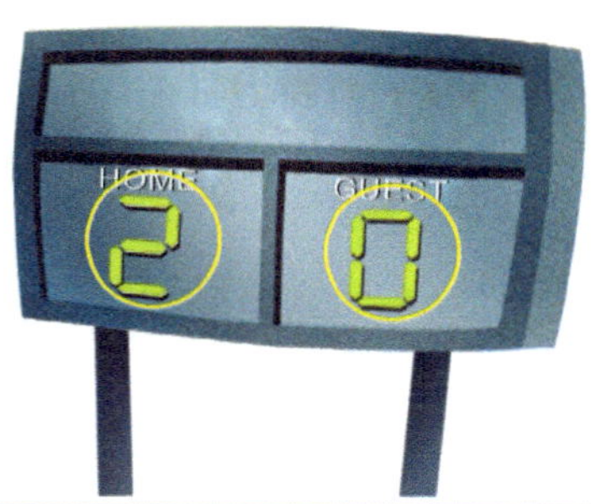

Let's Practice

1. What is the **function** of the number in each picture? Color the correct answer. Identify

a.

ordinal

nominal

cardinal

b.

ordinal

nominal

cardinal

c.

ordinal

nominal

cardinal

d.

ordinal

nominal

cardinal

Quiz Yourself

Analyze the picture and answer.

- If  passes two runners before reaching the finish line, which place will she finish in?

- What is the function of the number on her shirt?

  The number on her shirt is ______________________

  ____

Let's Check!

Counting, Reading and Representing Numbers Up To 20

1. Write the numbers your teacher reads out loud.

a. ☐ **b.** ☐ **c.** ☐ **d.** ☐

2. Write the number represented in each case.

a.

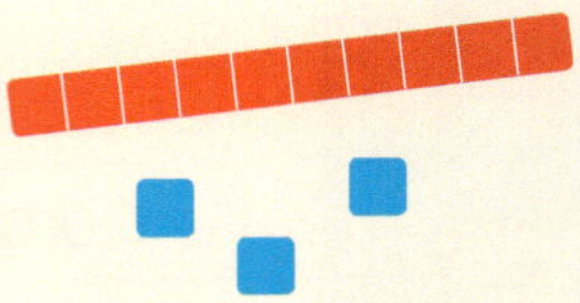

☐

b.

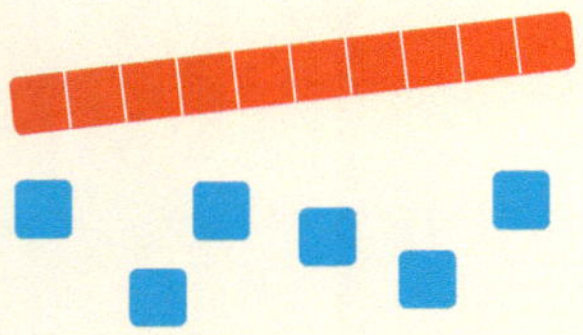

☐

c.

☐

3. Circle the amount of objects represented by each number.

a.

11

b.

15

c.

14

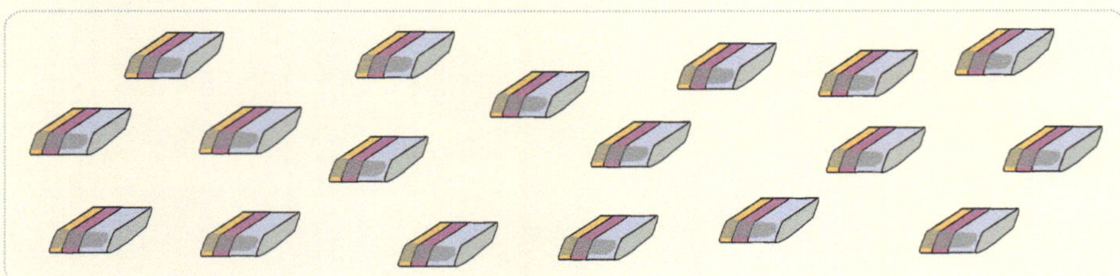

Comparing and Putting Numbers Up To 20 in Order

4. Order the numbers from the **least** to the **greatest**.

a. 12 9 13 ▶ ☐ ☐ ☐

b. 19 16 15 ▶ ☐ ☐ ☐

c. 11 20 10 ▶ ☐ ☐ ☐

Identify the Different Functions of Numbers

5. Use the hints to color the numbers in the image.

ordinal numbers

nominal numbers

cardinal numbers

How Did You Do?

For each color a .

Section 3

Numbers Up To 50

Counting, Reading and Representing

Let's Connect

- How many marbles has  counted?

  ☐

- How many more marbles does she have to count?

  ☐

- What number comes after 19?

  ☐

Let's Learn

10	and	10	20	twenty
20	and	10	30	thirty
30	and	10	40	forty
40	and	10	50	fifty

Tip

It's easier to count big numbers if you make groups of tens.

Let's Practice

1. Write the number of  in each case. Represent

a.

b.

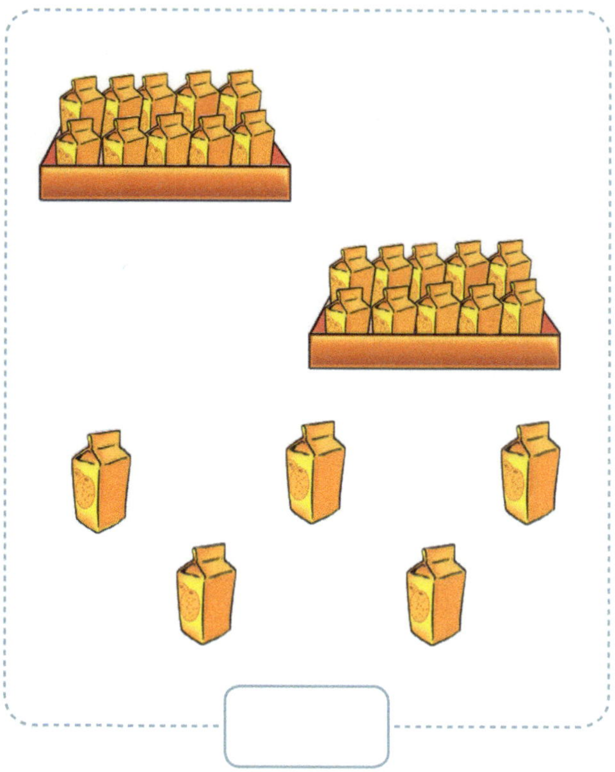

c.

d.

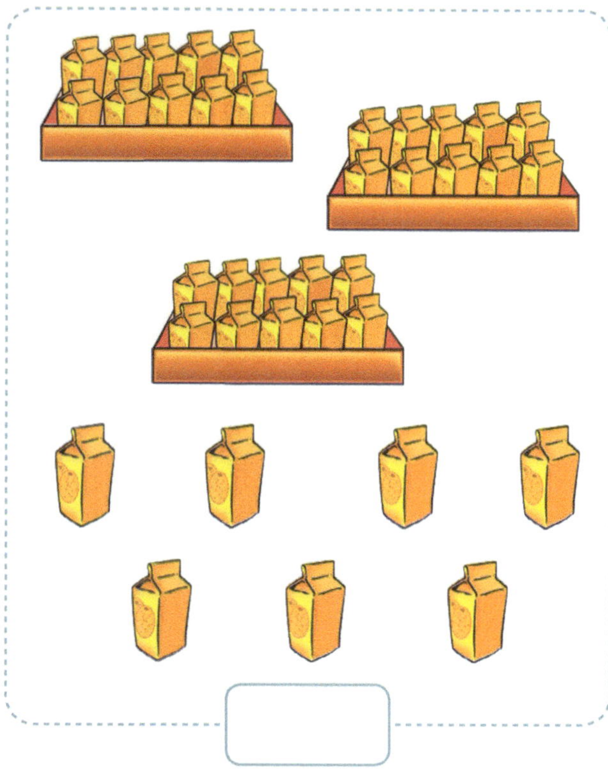

2. Represent each number using **Sticker Set 6** on **page 171.** Represent

a. 21

c. 27

b. 43

d. 32

3. Count the ● and write the corresponding number. Apply

You can **cross out** the dots as you count.

a.

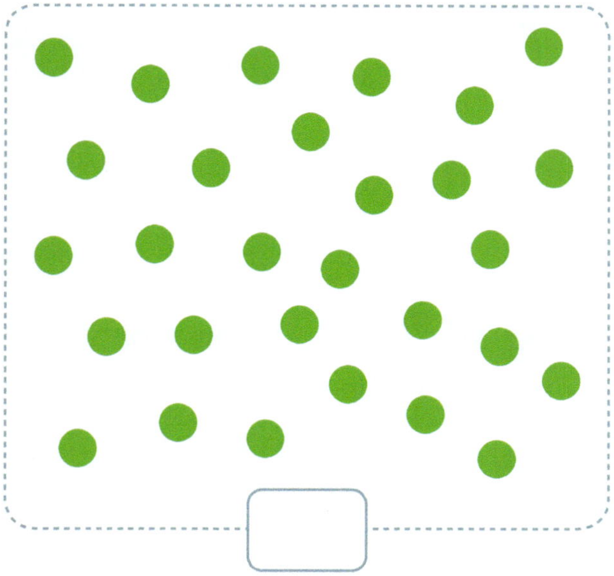

c.

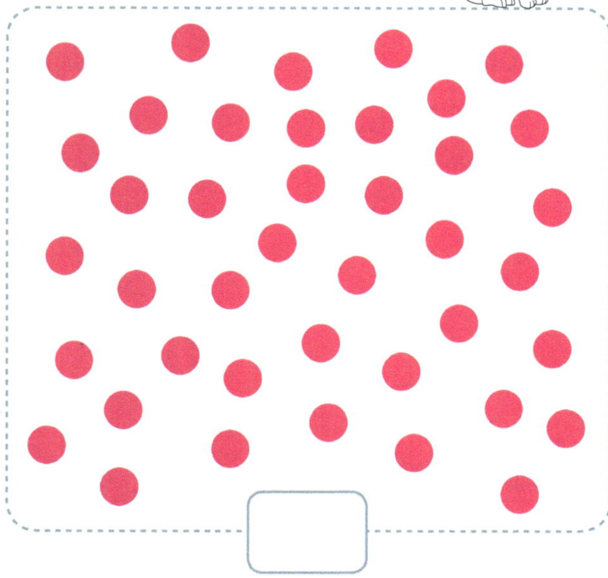

b.

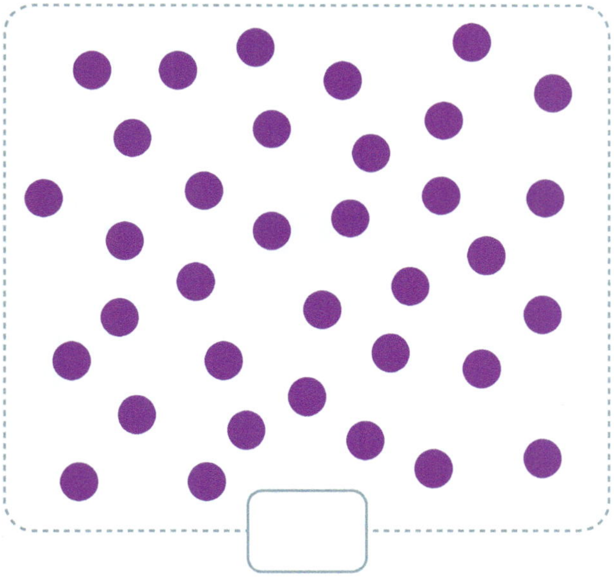

d.

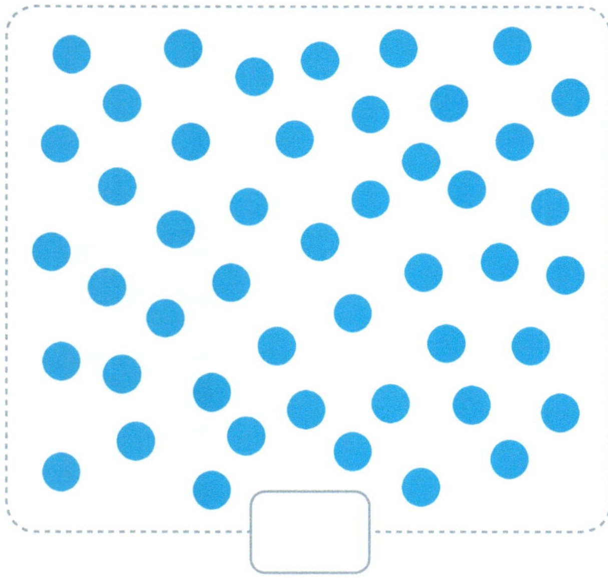

Did You Know...?

There are **even** and **odd** numbers.

- **Even** numbers can be divided into two equal groups. They end in 0, 2, 4, 6 or 8.
- **Odd** numbers cannot be divided into two equal groups. They end in 1, 3, 5, 7 or 9.

Challenge

Try forming two groups with your whole class.

- Is there an **even** or **odd** number of students in your class?
- How many different groups can you form?

Counting by Grouping

Let's Connect

- If  counted his marbles one by one, how did  count them?

  By ☐.

- How will  count his groups? Write the numbers in the boxes.

  5, ☐, ☐, ☐

Let's Learn

Grouping in different quantities makes **counting** easier.

By twos (2s)

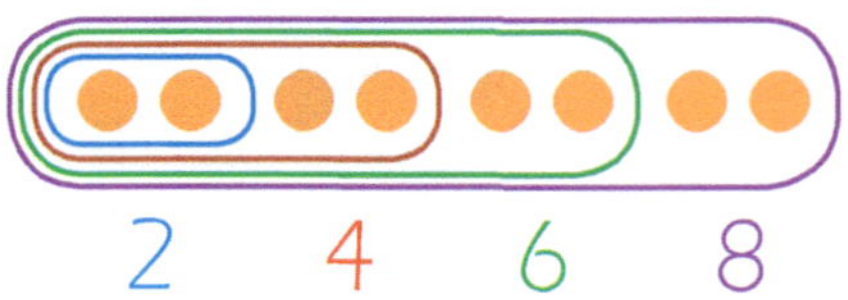

By fives (5s)

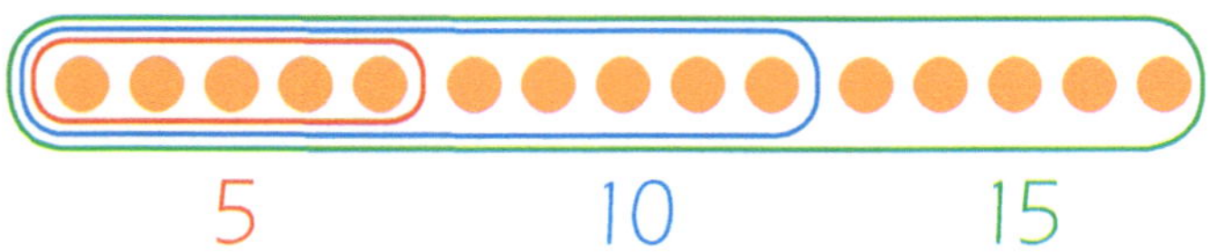

By tens (10s)

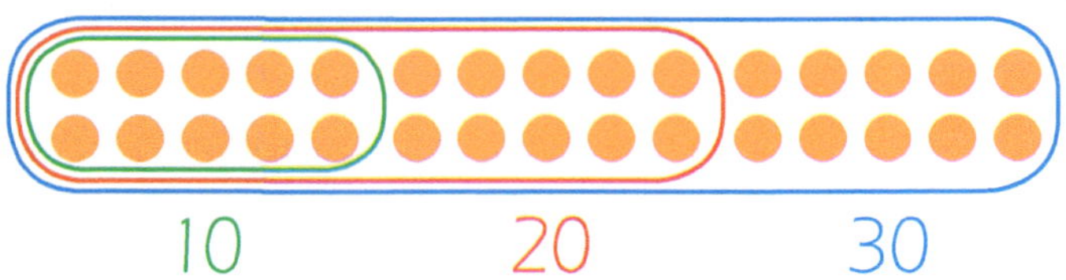

Fun Fact!

Games with marbles have been played for over two thousand years!

Let's Practice

1. Count the total number of ●. Circle by 2s or 5s. Apply

by twos (2s)

a.

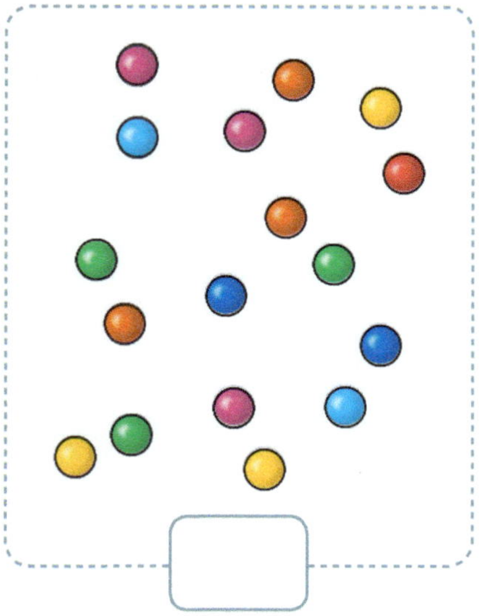

b.

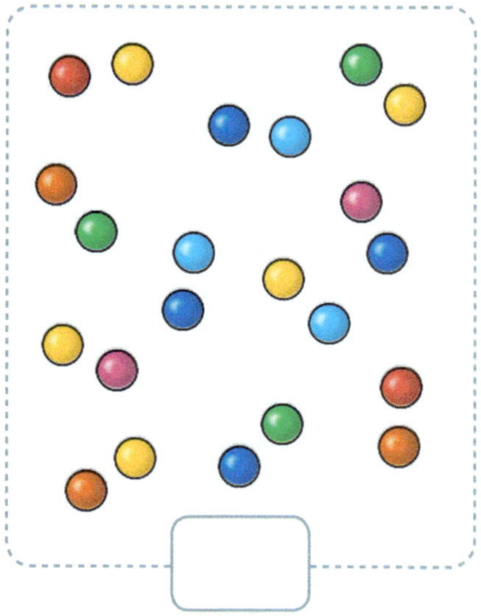

by fives (5s)

c.

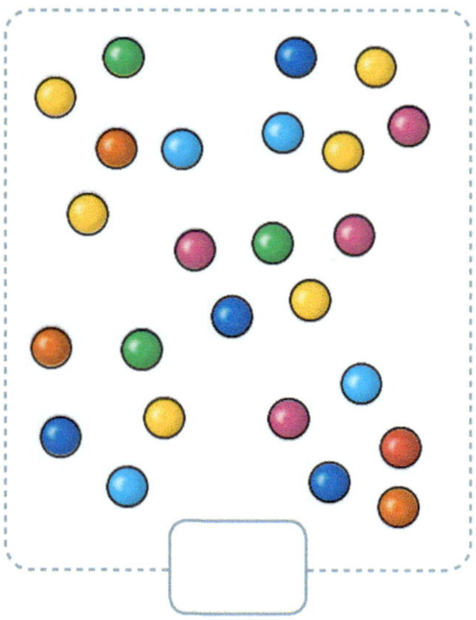

d.

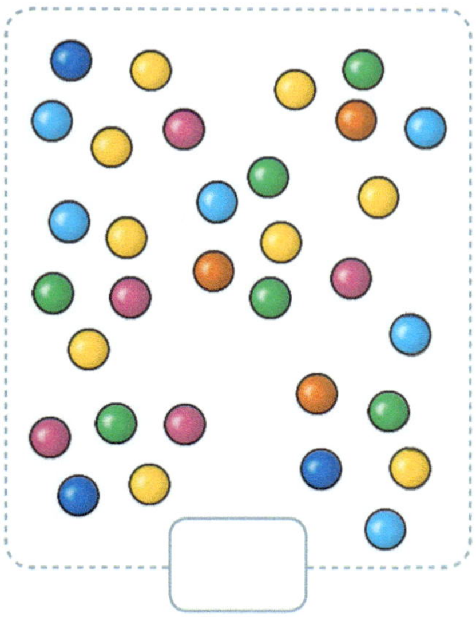

Did You Know...?

Circling groups of objects helps keep track of your counting.

Use the number chart on **Activity Card 7** to help you count.

Quiz Yourself

Count out loud with your classmates. Apply

- by twos, from 0 to 30
- by fives, from 0 to 30
- by tens, from 0 to 50

Section
4 Decimal Number System

Tens and Ones

Let's Connect

- How many blocks make 1 group of tens? Count them and write the quantity.

- How many blocks are there in total in the image?

- If you take away 1 ten, how many blocks are **left over**?

Let's Learn

A group of 10 **ones** is called 1 **ten**.

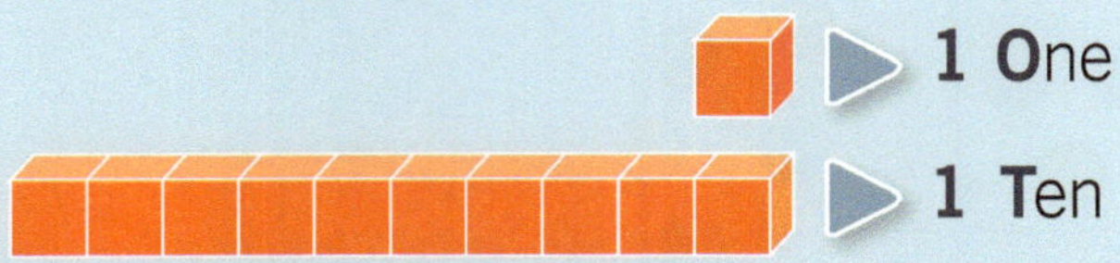

1 ten is equal to **10** ones
1 T = 10 O

T	O
1	5

1 T and 5 O equal 15 ones.

Did You Know...?

Numbers can be represented in a place value chart.

T	O
2	3

Let's Practice

1. Make 1 ten in each box using **Sticker Set 7** on **page 171**. Represent

a.

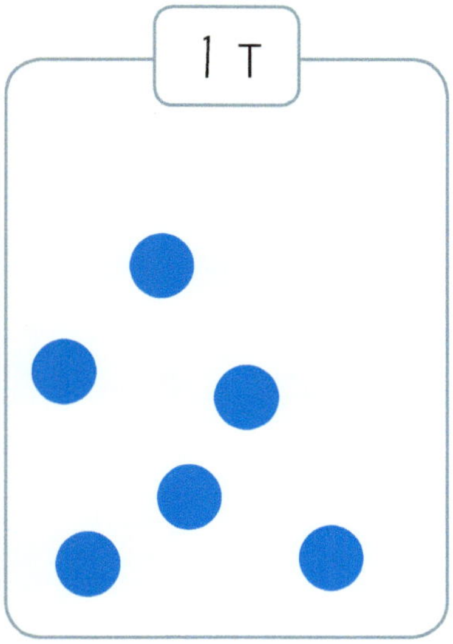

b.

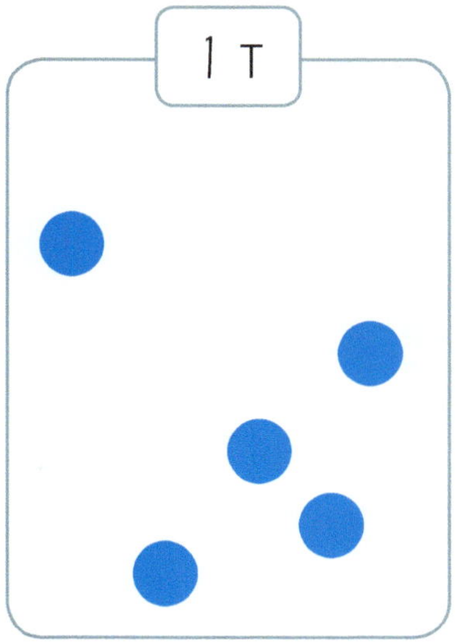

c.

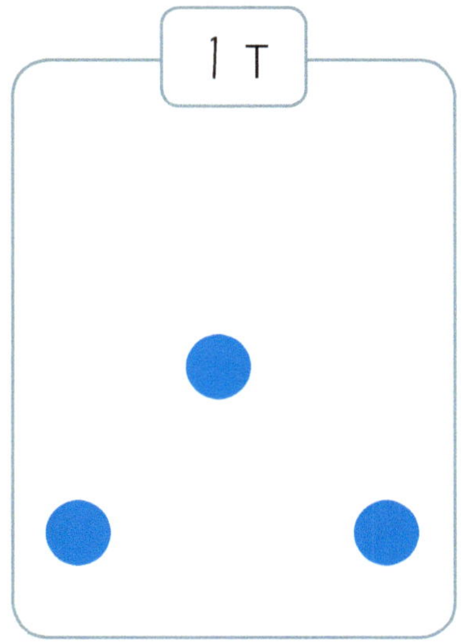

2. Complete with the correct number of tens. Interpret

a. 20 O equals ☐ T.

b. 40 O equals ☐ T.

c. ☐ O equals 5 T.

d. ☐ O equals 3 T.

3. Look at the example. Complete. Interpret

12 ▶ [1] T + [2] O

a. 38 ▶ ☐ T + ☐ O

b. 26 ▶ ☐ T + ☐ O

c. 44 ▶ ☐ T + ☐ O

d. 17 ▶ ☐ T + ☐ O

e. 33 ▶ ☐ T + ☐ O

f. 49 ▶ ☐ T + ☐ O

Place Value

Let's Connect

- What is the **place** of each digit on the board? Complete.

T	O

T	O

- What is the **place value** of 2 in both numbers?

21 ▶ ☐ ones   12 ▶ ☐ ones

- In which place does the digit 2 have a greater value? Circle.

ones   tens

Let's Learn

The **place value** of a **digit** depends on its **place** in the number.

T	O
1	2

▶ Here, 2 has a place value of **2 ones** because it is in the **ones place**.

T	O
2	1

▶ Here, 2 has a place value of **20 ones** or **2 tens** because it is in the **tens place**.

Let's Practice

1. Write the **place value** of each digit. Identify

a.

T	O
1	5
↓	↓
☐	☐

b.

T	O
3	3
↓	↓
☐	☐

c.

T	O
4	8
↓	↓
☐	☐

2. Complete. Interpret

a. In the number 46, the place value of 4 is ☐ ones.

b. In the number 23, the place value of 2 is ☐ ones.

c. In the number 10, the place value of 1 is ☐ ones.

d. In the number 35, the place value of 5 is ☐ ones.

3. Look at the underlined digits and circle the number with the smaller place value. Analyze

a. 4<u>1</u> <u>1</u>7

b. <u>2</u>3 4<u>2</u>

c. 4<u>3</u> <u>3</u>4

4. Circle the numbers with a **tens** value **greater** than 20 ones. Analyze

41 21 40 17

22 32 14 46

Decomposing Numbers

Let's Connect

- How many blocks does  have?

  ☐

- How many tens and ones does the number above have?

  ☐ tens ☐ ones

- What is the place value of each digit in this number? Complete.

T	O

↓ ☐ ↓ ☐

Decompose means to separate a number into parts.

Let's Learn

We can **decompose** numbers based on the **place value** of each digit.

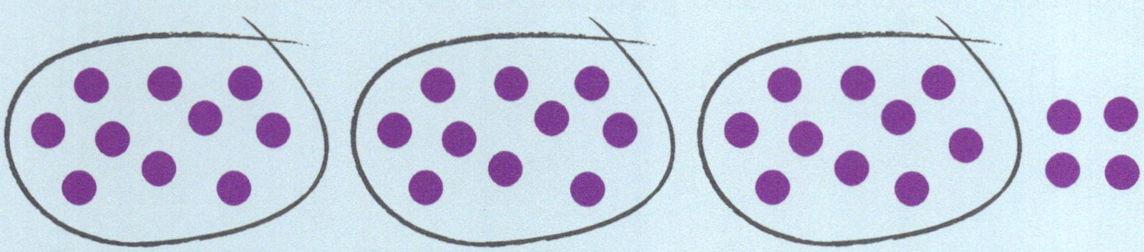

T	O
3	4

▶ 3 T and 4 O ▶ 30 + 4 ▶ 34

Let's Practice

1. Circle groups of tens. Write the number of ○ and the number of tens and ones. Apply

a.

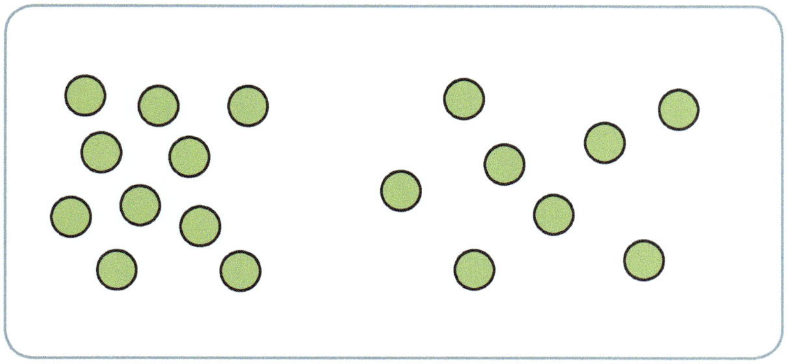

☐ ▶ ☐ T and ☐ O

b.

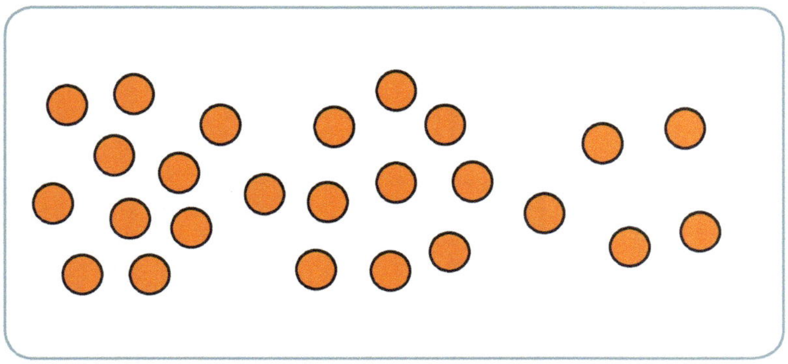

☐ ▶ ☐ T and ☐ O

c.

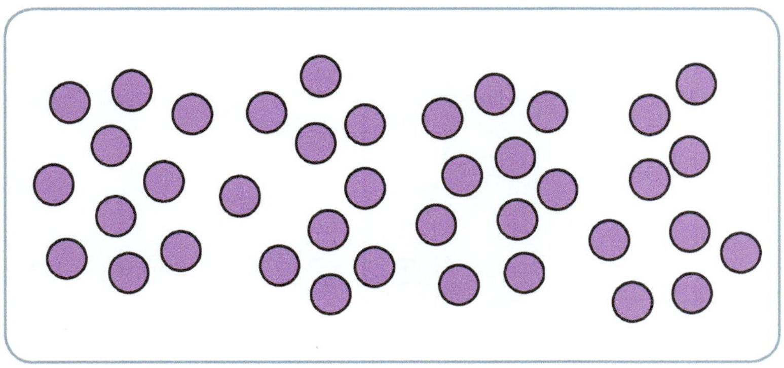

☐ ▶ ☐ T and ☐ O

d.

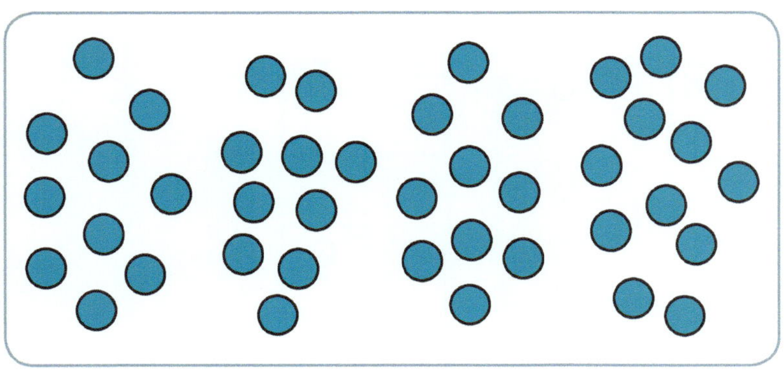

☐ ▶ ☐ T and ☐ O

2. Look at the example and **decompose** each number. Apply

T	O
4	1

▶ [4] T and [1] O ▶ [40] + [1]

a.

T	O
1	7

▶ [ ] T and [ ] O ▶ [ ] + [ ]

b.

T	O
3	2

▶ [ ] T and [ ] O ▶ [ ] + [ ]

c.

T	O
2	9

▶ [ ] T and [ ] O ▶ [ ] + [ ]

3. Look at the example and compose each number. Complete. Apply

[10] + [2] ▶ [1] T and [2] O ▶

T	O
1	2

a. [40] + [7] ▶ [ ] T and [ ] O ▶

T	O

b. [20] + [3] ▶ [ ] T and [ ] O ▶

T	O

c. [30] + [5] ▶ [ ] T and [ ] O ▶

T	O

4. Decompose each number. Apply

a. 15 ▸ ☐ + ☐

b. 27 ▸ ☐ + ☐

c. 36 ▸ ☐ + ☐

d. 48 ▸ ☐ + ☐

Quiz Yourself

Look at the picture and answer.

- Who is correct? Justify your answer by representing the quantity.

Exam Strategies

Look and Learn

Mark the correct answer with an ✕ .

Read the instructions. They tell you how to answer the question.

1 The quantities below represent the score of two teams in a basketball game.

Sometimes, there is information before the question. Read this carefully.

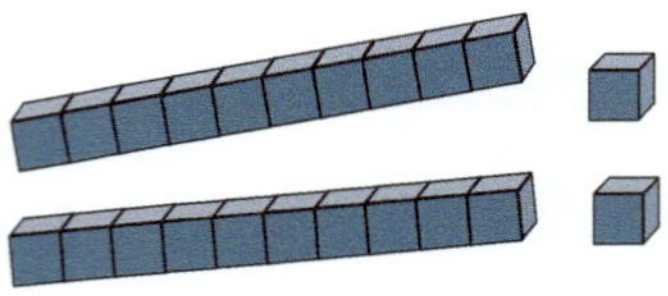

Team 1

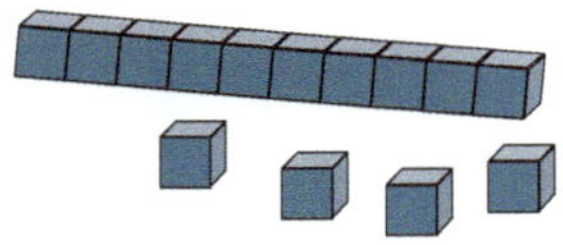

Team 2

Which team has the **higher** score?

Now read and understand the question. Find the correct strategy. You can reread the question to find important information.

☒ A Team 1

B Team 2

Find the correct answer. Mark it with an ✕.

Your Turn!

A strategy is a work plan, a way to get to your answer.

Mark the correct answer with an ✕ .

2 Michael is 43 years old.

Which one shows Michael's age correctly?

A 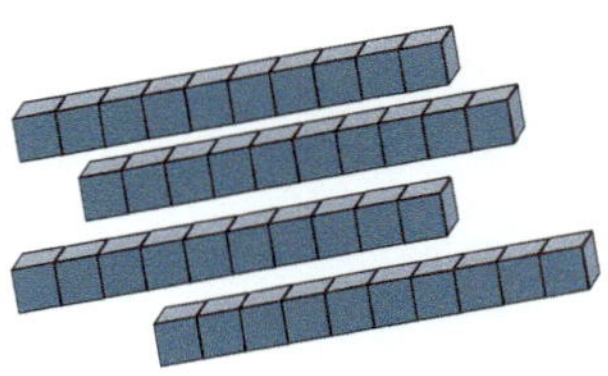

B 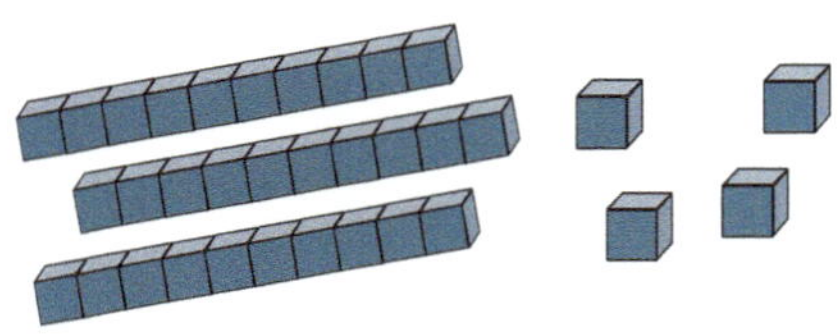

What Did You Learn?

Final Evaluation

Counting, Reading and Representing Numbers Up To 50

1. Group the ● by twos. Count and write the number.

a.

b.

Functions of Numbers

2. Match the numbers in the pictures with their functions.

ordinal

nominal

cardinal

3. Circle groups of tens. Write the number of ●, the number of tens and the number of ones.

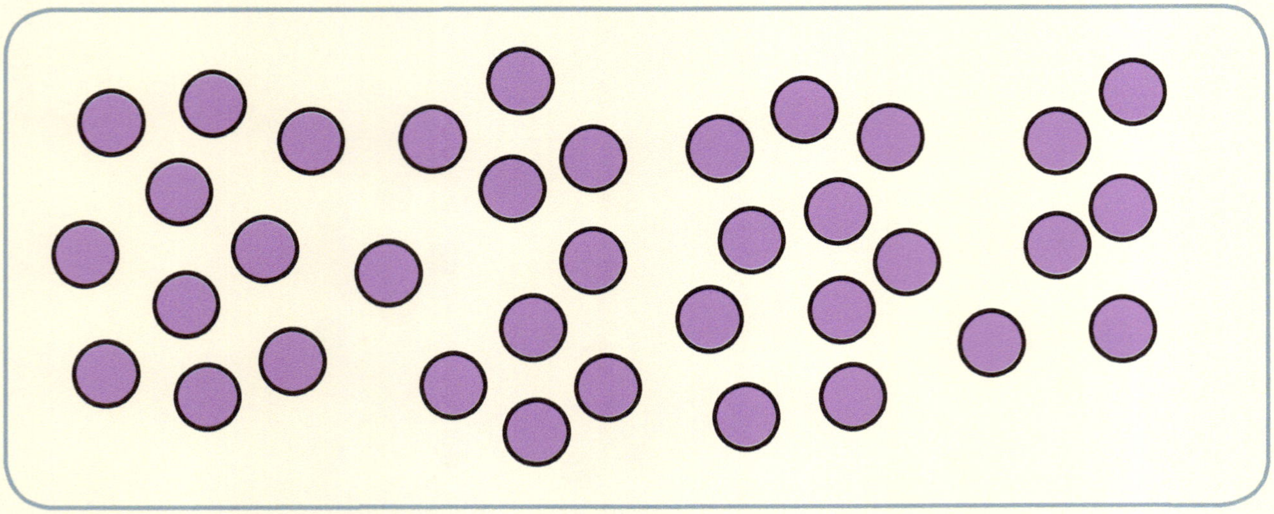

☐ ▶ ☐ T and ☐ O

Comparing and Putting Numbers Up To 50 in Order

4. Put the numbers in order from the greatest to the least.

48 22 36 ▶ ☐ ☐ ☐

Ones, Tens, Place Value and Decomposing Numbers

5. Complete.

	number	ones and tens	decomposition
a.	48	☐ T and ☐ O	☐ + ☐
b.	☐	2 T and 5 O	☐ + ☐
c.	☐	☐ T and ☐ O	30 + 2

Mark the correct answer with an ✕ .

6. Look at the numbers.

49 39

Which digit has the **higher place value**?

A 4

B 9

7. A lady is selling candles at a fair.

How many blue candles are for sale?

A 18

B 20

Find Test 2 Study Page

How Did You Do?

For each happy frog face color a lily pad.

Operations with Numbers Up To 50

Key Words

mental math

opposite

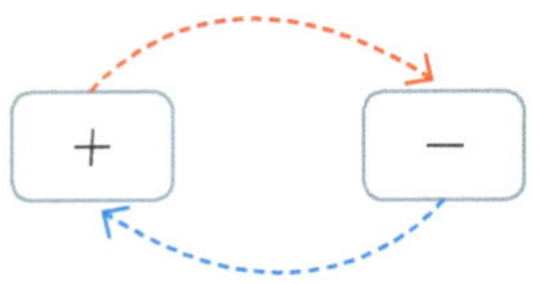

between

change

In this unit you will learn to:

- use written and mental math strategies to solve addition and subtraction problems and represent the process using pictures and symbols.
- understand the relationship between addition and subtraction.
- create and solve word problems.
- be organized and follow steps to solve a word problem.
- express ideas and listen to other ideas respectfully.

What Do You Know? Initial Evaluation

Look at the picture and answer.

1. Circle.

 numbers that order (ordinal numbers)
 numbers that identify (nominal numbers)

2. How many  are in **each** box?

There are [ ]  in **each** box.

3. How many **groups of 10**  are in the picture?

There are [ ] **groups of 10**  .

4. How much fruit is there **in all**?

There are [ ]  and  .

5. If **2 groups of 10**  are sold, how many are left over?

There are [ ]  left over.

Addition and Subtraction

The Relationship between Addition and Subtraction

Let's Connect

- What addition problem can you make from the three cards? Complete.

  ☐ + ☐ = ☐

- What subtraction problem can you make from the three cards? Complete.

  ☐ – ☐ = ☐

Let's Learn

Subtraction is the **opposite** or **inverse** of **addition**.

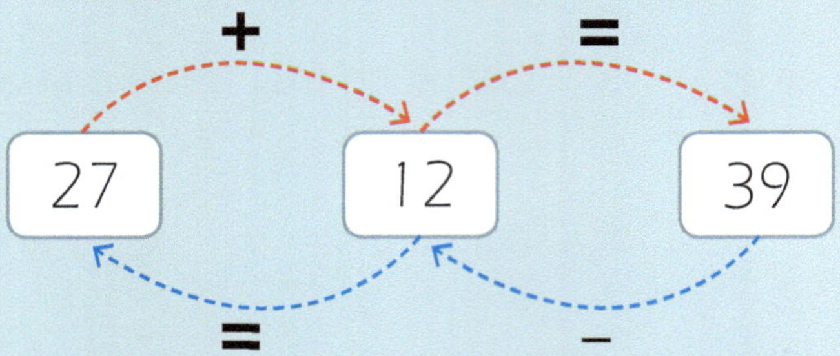

Word Focus

The **inverse** is the **opposite** of something. For example, dark is the opposite of light and clean is the opposite of dirty.

- The answer to an **addition** problem can be **proven** or **checked** using a subtraction operation. To **prove** or **check** means to show something is **true**.

$$27 + 12 = 39 \quad \text{so} \quad \begin{cases} 39 - 12 = 27 \\ 39 - 27 = 12 \end{cases}$$

- The answer to a **subtraction** problem can be **proven** or **checked** using an addition operation.

$$39 - 12 = 27 \quad \text{so} \quad \begin{cases} 27 + 12 = 39 \\ 12 + 27 = 39 \end{cases}$$

Let's Practice

1. Use the numbers in the boxes to write an addition operation and a subtraction operation. Apply

a. 6 | 49 | 43

☐ + ☐ = ☐

☐ − ☐ = ☐

b. 45 | 12 | 33

☐ + ☐ = ☐

☐ − ☐ = ☐

Quiz Yourself

Read the problem and answer.

Emily and Matt collected  to donate to a recycling campaign. Matt collected 25 and Emily collected the rest.

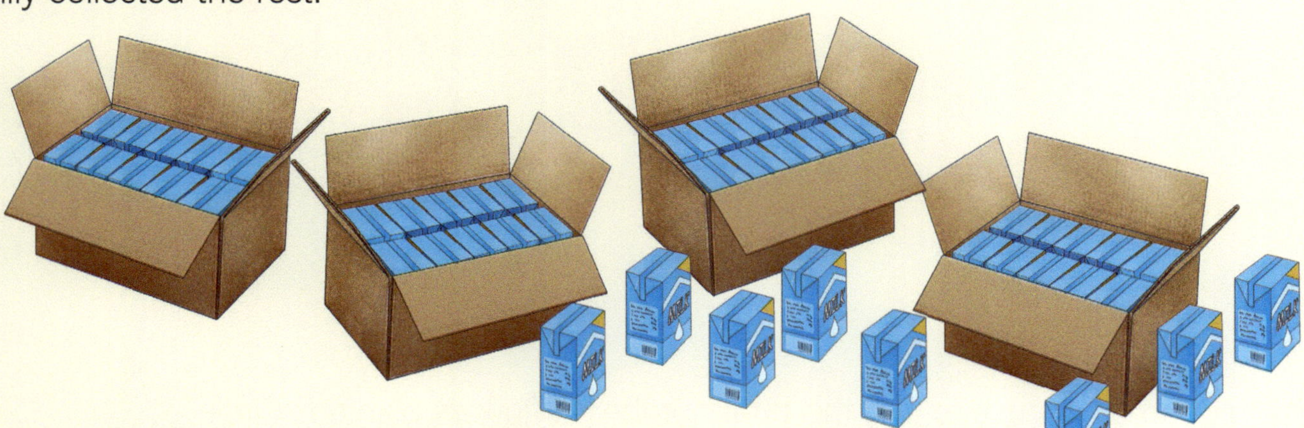

- How many  did Emily collect? Write the operation and the answer.

☐ ☐ ☐ = ☐

- Check your answer.

☐ ☐ ☐ = ☐

Combination Word Problems

Let's Connect

- What **action** do we use to find the **total** number of flowers planted? Circle.

combine take away

- What **operation** is related to this **action**? Circle.

addition subtraction

- How many flowers are they planting **in all**? ☐

Let's Learn

Combination word problems are related to the actions of **combining** and **separating**.

15  and 12  were planted in a garden.

How many flowers were planted in all?

To solve this problem, look at:

The information:	15  and 12 .
The question:	How many flowers were planted in all?
The **action** used to solve the problem:	combine
The **operation** used to solve the problem:	addition

With this information you can:

Write the operation and solve:	15 + 12 = 27
Answer:	27 flowers were planted in all.
Check or **prove** your answer:	27 − 15 = 12 27 − 12 = 15

Remember!

You can check your answer using the relationship between addition and subtraction.

Let's Practice

1. Underline the information and question. Then circle the correct action. Interpret

information question

a. Christina used 30  and 20  to make a necklace.

How many  does Christina's necklace have in all?

Action: combine take away

b. John has a collection of 15 .

12 of these  are **small** and the rest are **big**.

How many big  does John have?

Action: combine take away

Fun Fact!

The spinning top is a very popular toy all around the world, but especially in Latin America.

2. Circle the **operation** that solves each problem. Interpret

a. Gabriel and Albert collect sports magazines. They have 40 magazines and 20 are Gabriel's. How many magazines does Albert have?

40 + 20 40 – 20

b. There are  and  in a garden. If there are 30  and 19 , how many flowers are there **in all**?

30 + 19 30 – 19

3. Solve. Analyze

a. Alex and Elliot are a team in a game of memory cards.
Alex wins 30 pairs of cards and Peter wins 14 pairs.
How many pairs did their team win **in all**?

Underline the **information** in orange.

Underline the **question** in blue.

Action: ____________________ **Operation:** ☐ ☐ ☐ = ☐

Answer: ____

Check: ☐ ☐ ☐ = ☐

b. There are 25 apples on a tree.
12 of the apples are ripe.
How many apples are not ripe?

Underline the **information** in orange.

Underline the **question** in blue.

Action: ____________________ **Operation:** ☐ ☐ ☐ = ☐

Answer: ____

Check: ☐ ☐ ☐ = ☐

Word Problems with a Change

Let's Connect

- After Daniela's donation, will there be **more** or **fewer** books? Circle.

    more books　　　　**fewer** books

- What **action** can you use to calculate the **total** number of books after Daniela's donation? Circle.

    remove　　　　add

- What operation is related to this action? Circle your answer.

    addition　　　　subtraction

- How many books are there after Daniela's donation? ☐

Word Focus

When you **donate** something, you give it away for free.

Let's Learn

Word problems with a **change** relate to the actions of **adding** or **removing**, or moving **forward** or **backward**.

A book fair collected 22  .

Daniela donates 25  .

How many  has the book fair collected in all?

We solve problems with a change in the same way we solve word problems that put things together. You should look at: the **information**, the **action** and the **operation** that will solve the problem. Then you can answer the question and check your answer.

Let's Practice

1. Write the operation that will solve each problem. Interpret

a.

☐ ☐ ☐ = ☐

b.

☐ ☐ ☐ = ☐

2. Solve the word problems. Analyze

a. Rose organized 34 books on a bookshelf.
Her friend Lucia gave her 10 **more** books to organize.
How many books are there on the bookshelf **in all**?

Underline the **information** in .

Underline the **question** in .

Action: ____________________ **Operation**: ☐ ☐ ☐ = ☐

Answer: ____

Check: ☐ ☐ ☐ = ☐

b. Charles had 28 pencils and then gave some to Louis.
Charles now has 21 pencils.
How many pencils did he give to Louis?

Underline the **information** in .

Underline the **question** in .

Action: ____________________ **Operation**: ☐ ☐ ☐ = ☐

Answer: ____

Check: ☐ ☐ ☐ = ☐

c. Peter and Camilo have collected 23 cans for a recycling campaign. Their friend Jorge gives them 6 more cans. How many cans do they have in all?

Underline the **information** in red.

Underline the **question** in blue.

Action: ______________________ **Operation:** ☐ ☐ ☐ = ☐

Answer: ____

Check: ☐ ☐ ☐ = ☐

d. Anna wants to go to 45 different cities. She visits 12 cities. How many more does she need to visit?

Underline the **information** in red.

Underline the **question** in blue.

Action: ______________________ **Operation:** ☐ ☐ ☐ = ☐

Answer: ____

Check: ☐ ☐ ☐ = ☐

Challenge

Act out the word problems from **a** and **b**.

Write a Word Problem

Let's Learn

To write a word problem, you should follow these steps:

1. Think about the **context** of the word problem.

   For example: *The number of tokens in a box.*

2. Decide which operation will solve the word problem.

   For example: *addition*

3. Decide on important information to present in the word problem.

   For example: *There are 23 red tokens and 23 green tokens.*

4. Decide on the right question for the word problem.

   For example: *How many tokens are there in total?*

5. Write the word problem.

   For example: *There are 23 red tokens and 23 green tokens in a box.*

   How many tokens are in the box in total?

Let's Practice

1. Write a word problem using the steps. Create

1st ▶ Write the context.

____

____

Word Focus

Context is the situation or condition.

2nd ▶ Circle the operation.

addition subtraction

3rd ▶ Write the information.

There are ______________________________

____

4th ▶ Write the question.

How many ______________________________

____

5th ▶ Write the word problem.

____

____

____

____

____

Quiz Yourself

Read the information and answer.

A deck of memory cards has 18 animal cards and 18 fruit cards.

Which question asks about a **change**? Circle.

How many cards are there in the deck in all?

If you take out the fruit cards, how many memory cards are left over?

Exam Strategies

Look and Learn

Mark the correct answer with an ✗.

This is a general instruction to answer the question.

Read the problem and answer questions 1 and 2.

In some cases, instructions apply to a **group** of questions.

Steven lives on the 22nd floor of a building.

He has to go down 11 floors to visit Camilla.

What floor does Camilla live on?

A text with facts gives you enough information to answer the questions.

1 Which **operation** is related to the problem?

A Addition.

☒ B Subtraction.

There are 2 questions that are answered by the same word problem.

2 Which operation solves the problem correctly?

☒ A $22 - 11 = 11$

B $22 + 11 = 33$

Each question has answer choices. Remember that you need to mark the correct answer with an ✗.

What Did You Learn?

Final Evaluation

Mental Math Strategies

1. Listen to the operations your teacher reads out loud. Write the answer.

a. ☐ **c.** ☐

b. ☐ **d.** ☐

Write Word Problems

2. Write a word problem using the following information.

Context: Petals is a flower shop.

Operation: subtraction

Information: 35 flowers in total and 23 roses.

Word problem:

____

____

____

____

____

____

____

____

Combination Word Problems and Word Problems with a Change

3. Solve the problems.

a. My mother gave me $25. Now I have $47. How much money did I have before?

Underline the information in .

Underline the question in .

Action: ______________________ **Operation:** ☐ ☐ ☐ = ☐

Answer: ____

Check: ☐ ☐ ☐ = ☐

b. Yesterday my photo album had 32 pictures. Today I added 16 more pictures. How many pictures are in my photo album now?

Underline the information in .

Underline the question in .

Action: ______________________ **Operation:** ☐ ☐ ☐ = ☐

Answer: ____

Check: ☐ ☐ ☐ = ☐

Mark the correct answer with an ✕.

Read the problem and answer questions 4 and 5.

Phillip has a story with **35** pages.
He reads **12** pages of the story.
How many pages are there left in the story?

4. What **action** is involved in this problem?

A Combine.

B Take away.

5. Which numbered tape shows the steps necessary to solve the problem?

A 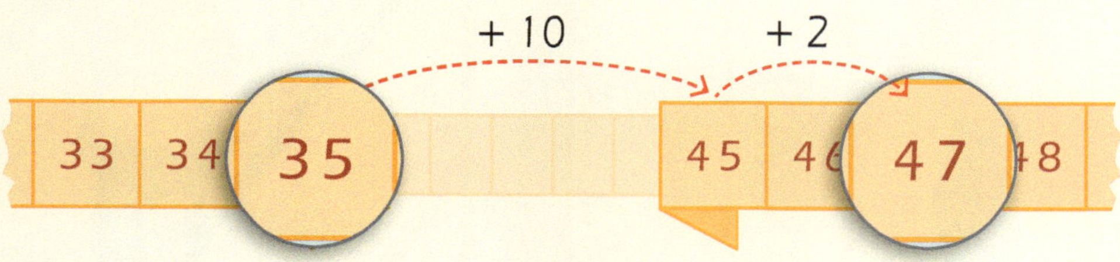

B 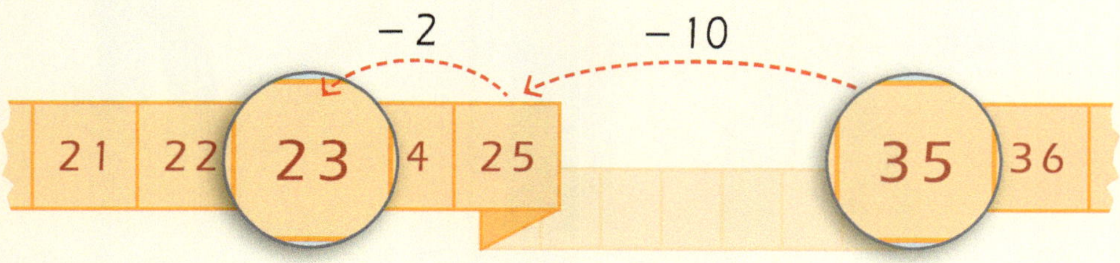

Find Test 3 Study Page

How Did You Do?

For each 🐸 color a ⬭.

Unit 4

Numbers and Operations Up To 100

Key Words

successor

50 ➡ 51

predecessor

50 ⬅ 51

In this unit you will learn to:

- count numbers up to 100, one by one and by grouping.
- recognize successors and predecessors of numbers up to 100.
- recognize ones and tens in numbers up to 100.
- determine the place value of digits in numbers.
- represent situations with addition and subtraction.
- solve addition and subtraction problems using composition and decomposition.
- be creative in finding solutions to math problems.

What Do You Know? Initial Evaluation

Look at the picture and answer.

1. How many players does each team have?

   The team has ☐ players.

   The team has ☐ players.

2. How many did the team knock down?

   ☐ .

3. 5 points are scored for each knocked down. How many points does the team have?

   ☐ points.

4. How many does the team have to knock down to win?

   ☐ .

Section 1

Numbers Up To 100

Let's Connect

rows →

columns ↓

30	31	32	33	34	35	36	37	38	39
40	41	42	43	44	45	46	47	48	49
50	51	52	53	54	55	56	57	58	59

Rows are **horizontal** ⊢⊣ and **columns** are **vertical** ⌶.

Mark the correct answer with an **X**.

- Look at the rows. The numbers are counted: one by one ☐ by tens ☐
- Look at the columns. The numbers are counted: one by one ☐ by tens ☐

Let's Learn

Number Chart

1. Use the table to count out loud by twos from 0 to 100. Then count out loud by tens from 0 to 100.

2. Color the numbers as you count by twos from 0 to 100. Discuss what you see with your class.

Challenge

Try counting by tens from 0 to 100 with your eyes closed. With a classmate, see who can count by tens without making a mistake.

0	1	2	3	4	5	6	7	8	9
10	11	12	13	14	15	16	17	18	19
20	21	22	23	24	25	26	27	28	29
30	31	32	33	34	35	36	37	38	39
40	41	42	43	44	45	46	47	48	49
50	51	52	53	54	55	56	57	58	59
60	61	62	63	64	65	66	67	68	69
70	71	72	73	74	75	76	77	78	79
80	81	82	83	84	85	86	87	88	89
90	91	92	93	94	95	96	97	98	99
100									

Let's Practice

1. Complete the sequence. Apply

- by **ones**

a.

50	51	52							

b.

90	91								

- by **tens**

c.

0	10	20							

d.

2	12	22							

2. Write the total amount of money. Apply

a.

b.

Counting by Grouping

Let's Connect

- How many **tokens** are in each tower? ☐
- How many **towers** are there in all? ☐
- How many tokens are there **in all**? ☐

Let's Learn

Counting in **groups of tens** helps you count large numbers.

There are 50 tokens.

Let's Practice

1. Write the total number of notebooks. Apply

a.

d.

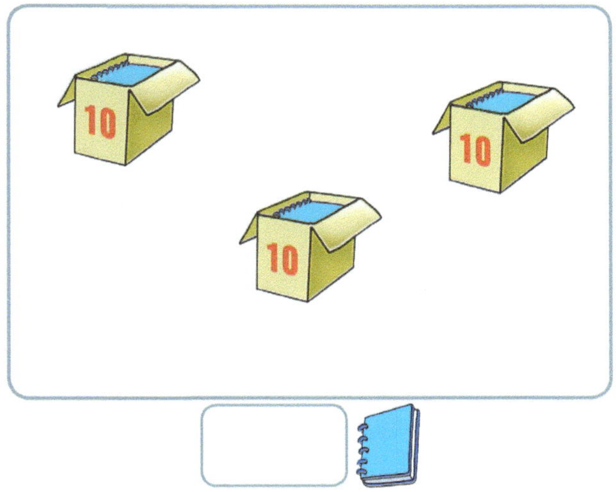

b.

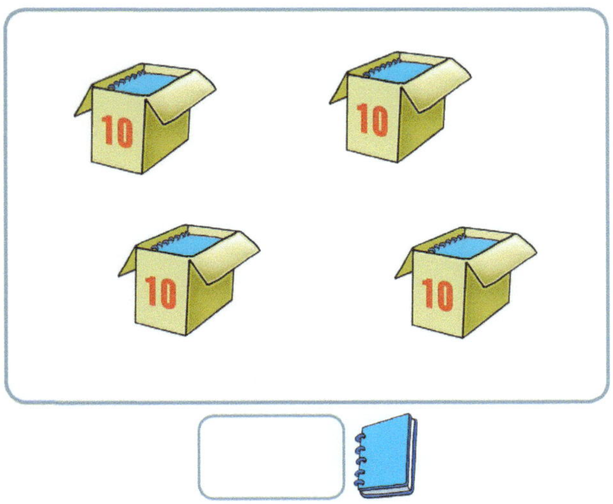

e.

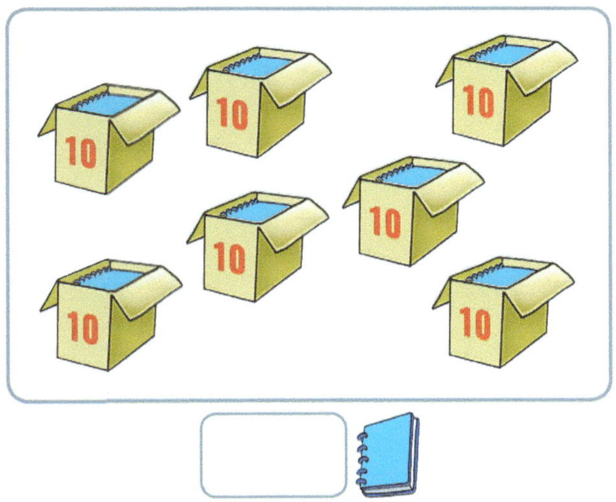

c.

f.

Predecessor and Successor

Let's Connect

- How many  does  have in all? ☐
-  **adds** one . How many cubes does he have? ☐
-  **subtracts** one . How many cubes does he have? ☐

Let's Learn

- The **predecessor** is **1 less than** the number.

predecessor ← **number**

T	O
4	4

T	O
4	5

- The **successor** is **1 greater than** the number.

number → **successor**

T	O
4	5

T	O
4	6

Word Focus

Predecessor means before or previous.
Successor means after or following.

Let's Practice

1. Write the **predecessor**. Apply

a. ☐

T	O
	5

b. ☐

T	O
1	8

c. ☐

T	O
4	9

2. Write the **successor**. Apply

a.

T	O
1	6

☐

b.

T	O
3	0

☐

c.

T	O
2	2

☐

3. Write the **predecessor** and the **successor**. Apply

a. ☐

T	O
1	5

☐

b. ☐

T	O
	9

☐

c. ☐

T	O
2	0

☐

d. ☐

T	O
3	6

☐

Quiz Yourself

Put the numbers in order.

- 26 28 27

predecessor ☐ number ☐ **successor** ☐

Decimal Number System

Tens and Ones

Let's Connect

50	51	52	53	54	55	56	57	58	59

- Which **digit** in each number **stays the same**?

____

- Which **digit** in each number **changes**?

____

Did You Know...?

Every known number uses just these ten digits:

0, 1, 2, 3, 4
5, 6, 7, 8, 9

Let's Learn

Numbers up to 100 are formed with **ones** (**O**) and **tens** (**T**).

10 O equals 1 T

There are **10 different numbers** that can be formed by changing the digit in the **ones** place when the digit in the **tens** place stays the same:

5 T and 0 O → 50
5 T and 1 O → 51
5 T and 2 O → 52
5 T and 3 O → 53
5 T and 4 O → 54

5 T and 5 O → 55
5 T and 6 O → 56
5 T and 7 O → 57
5 T and 8 O → 58
5 T and 9 O → 59

Let's Practice

1. Complete the table with the numbers formed by tens and ones. Do the activities. Apply

	0 O	1 O	2 O	3 O	4 O	5 O	6 O	7 O	8 O	9 O
0 T	0	1	2	3	4	5				
1 T	10	11								
2 T			22							
3 T						35				
4 T					44					
5 T									58	
6 T							66			
7 T		71								
8 T	80									
9 T										99

a. Color the numbers formed with 8 T in .

b. Color the numbers formed with 4 O in .

c. Color the **predecessors** of the numbers formed with 7 O .

Place Value

Let's Connect

- What numbers can you form with the digits shown by the cards?
- In which **number** does 8 have the **place value** of 8 ones?
- In which **number** does 8 have the **place value** of 80 ones?

Let's Learn

The **value** of a digit depends on its **position** in the number. This is called its **place value**.

T	O
7	8

The digit has the **place** value of 8 ones because it is in the **ones place**.

T	O
8	7

The digit has the **place** value of 80 ones or 8 tens because it is in the **tens place**.

Did You Know...?

The **decimal numbering system** is a positional system. The value of each digit depends on its place in the number.

Let's Practice

1. Write the **place value** of the digits in each number. Identify

a.

T	O
5	8

⬇ ⬇ ☐ ☐

b.

T	O
6	3

⬇ ⬇ ☐ ☐

c.

T	O
8	1

⬇ ⬇ ☐ ☐

2. Circle the correct answers. Interpret

a. The **digit** 5 has a **place value** of 5 ones.

45 59 95 51

b. The **digit** 4 has a **place value** of 40 ones.

49 43 94 74

c. The **digit** 7 has a **place value** of 70 ones.

47 78 71 57

3. Look at the numbers and answer. Apply

73 38

a. Circle the digit that appears in both numbers.

b. What **place value** does this digit have?

In 73 it has a place value of ➡ ☐ ones.

In 38 it has a place value of ➡ ☐ ones.

Composing and Decomposing Numbers Using Addition

Let's Connect

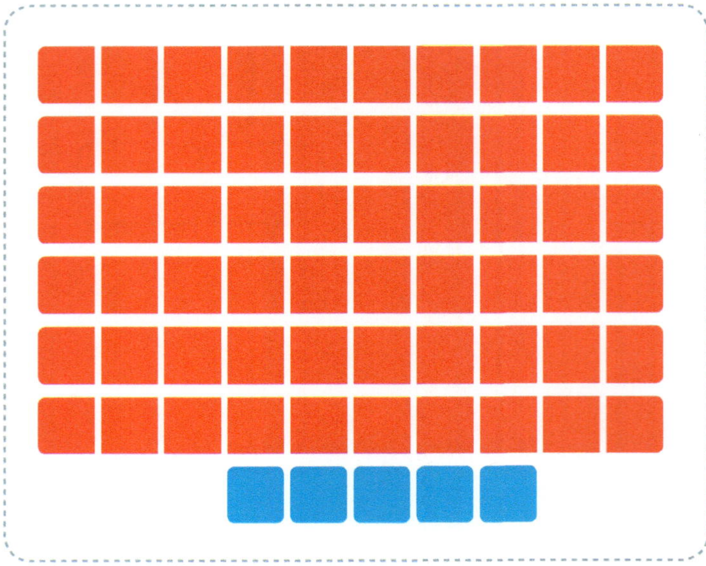

- What number does this represent?

- Write the number in the box with the correct digits in the **tens** and **ones** place. Write the **place value** of each digit.

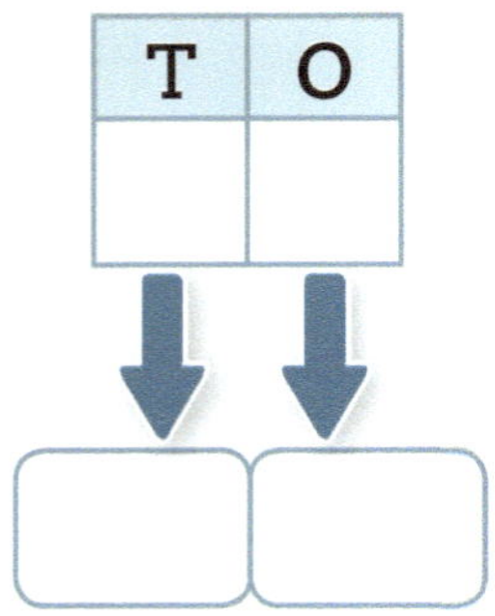

Let's Learn

- You can solve addition operations with the **composition** or **decomposition** of numbers.

65

↓

can be **composed**

- according to the **name** of its position:

6 T + 5 O

- by **place value**:

60 + 5

60 + 5

or

6 T + 5 O

↓

becomes

65

Using **composition**.

Let's Practice

1. **Compose** each number. Apply

a. 3 T + 3 O

b. 8 T + 9 O

c. 70 + 6

d. 90 + 4

2. **Decompose** each number according to the **name** of its position. Apply

a. 48

☐ T + ☐ O

b. 62

☐ T + ☐ O

c. 57

☐ T + ☐ O

3. **Decompose** each number according to its **place value**. Apply

a. 19

☐ + ☐

b. 51

☐ + ☐

c. 86

☐ + ☐

Quiz Yourself

Look at the cards and answer.

- What is the **greatest** number that can be formed with the cards?

- What is the **smallest** number that can be formed with the cards?

Let's Check!

Numbers Up To 100

1. Write the total number of notebooks.

a.

b.

Predecessors and Successors

2. Write the predecessor and successor of each number.

a.

T	O
4	9

b.

T	O
7	5

Ones and Tens, Place Value, Composing and Decomposing Numbers

3. Write the number represented in each case.

a.

b.

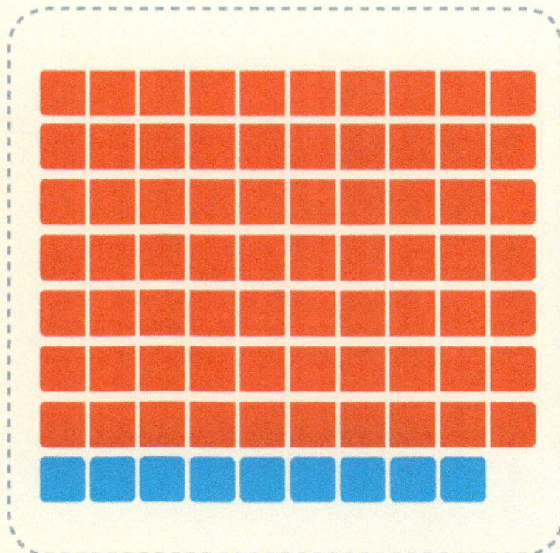

4. Write the numbers from 3 with the correct digits in the tens and ones places. Then decompose the numbers.

☐ T + ☐ O
☐ + ☐

☐ T + ☐ O
☐ + ☐

How Did You Do?

For each (frog) color a (lily pad).

Section
3 Addition and Subtraction

Comparisons

Let's Connect

- How many ice cream sticks does each child have?

 ☐  ☐

- Circle the child who has **more** ice cream sticks.

- How many ice cream sticks should  **add** or **subtract** to have the same amount as ? Use **Sticker Set 8** on **page 171** to represent the quantity.

add	subtract

Let's Learn

Comparing is related to **addition** and **subtraction**.

We **compare** when we look for the **difference** between two quantities.

$60 - 40 = 20$

 has 20 **more** sticks than .

 has 20 **fewer** sticks than .

We also compare when we know one of the quantities and the difference.

$60 - 20 = 40$

 has 40 sticks.

$40 + 20 = 60$

 has 60 sticks.

Let's Practice

1. Compare the quantities. Write the operation and answer. Apply

a. How many **more** sticks does  have than  ?

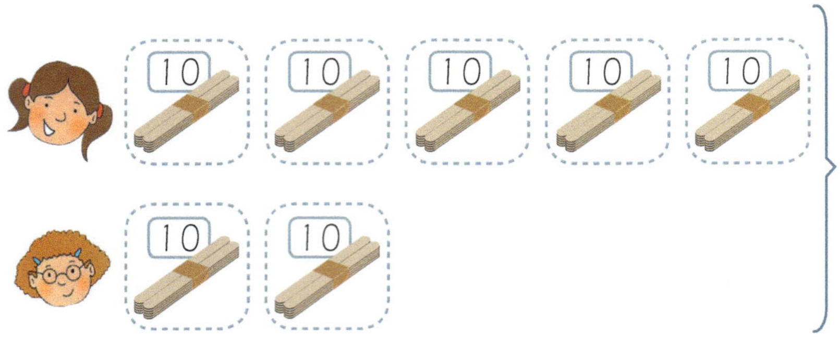

____ ____ ____ = ____

 has ____ **more** sticks than .

b. How many **fewer** bags does  have than  ?

____ ____ ____ = ____

 has ____ **fewer** bags than .

c. How many fewer squares does **B** have than **A**?

A

B

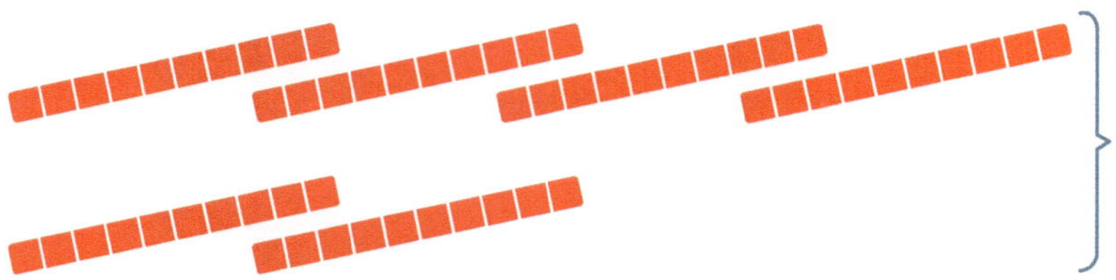

____ ____ ____ = ____

B has ____ **fewer** squares than **A**.

2. Use **Sticker Set 9** on **page 171** to represent each situation.

a.

• How many marbles does have?

has marbles.

=

b.

• How many marbles does have?

has marbles.

=

Addition with More Than Two Addends

Let's Connect

- How many sticks does each girl have?

-  and  add their sticks together. How many sticks do they have in total?
-  adds her sticks to the other girls'. How many sticks do they have in total?

Let's Learn

To solve an **addition operation with three addends**, add two of the addends first. Then add the third addend.

$$15 + 11 + 12$$
$$26 + 12$$
$$38$$

Let's Practice

1. Solve. Apply

a. 22 + 14 + 10

☐ + 10

☐

b. 15 + 20 + 33

☐ + 33

☐

Quiz Yourself

Read and answer.

- How many marbles does Roddy have?

Roddy has ☐ marbles.

Comparison Word Problems

Let's Connect

- What did  do to find the number of pictures he has in his album? Color.

  ◯ He counted the number of pictures.

  ◯ He estimated the number of pictures.

  ◯ He compared the number of pictures.

Challenge

Compare your stickers, pencils or other items with a friend's. Who has more? Write the operations.

- Which operation can be used to find the number of pictures  has in his album? Circle.

  46 + 22   46 − 22

- How many pictures does  have in his album?

  ☐ ☐ ☐ = ☐

   has ☐ pictures in his album.

Let's Learn

We can **compare** to solve **comparison** word problems.

 has 46 pictures.  has 22 more pictures than .

How many pictures does  have?

As with composition and change word problems, to solve a comparison word problem, you should also consider:

Information	46 pictures and 22 more pictures.
Question	How many pictures does  have?
Action	compare

Decide whether the information asks for a **sum** or a **difference**. This will help you decide which operation to use to solve the problem.

Operation	addition

With this information you can:

Write the operation and find the answer.	$46 + 22 = 68$
Give an answer.	 has 68 pictures in his album.
Check your answer.	$68 - 22 = 46$

Let's Practice

1. Solve the following problems. Analyze

a. Robert's grandmother is 73 years old. His grandfather is 5 years **older** than his grandmother. How old is Robert's grandfather?

Underline the information in orange.

Underline the question in blue.

Operation:

T	O

Answer: ______________________

Check your answer: ☐ ☐ ☐ = ☐

b. There are 67 tokens in the box. There are 45 **fewer** tokens in the jar than there are in the box. How many tokens are there in the jar?

Underline the information in orange.

Underline the question in blue.

Operation:

T	O

Answer: ______________________

Check your answer: ☐ ☐ ☐ = ☐

c. Gabriel picked 78 apples. Mark picked 54 apples. How many fewer apples did Mark pick?

Underline the information in orange.

Underline the question in blue.

Operation:

T	O

Answer: ______________________________

Check your answer: ☐ ☐ ☐ = ☐

d. On Saturday 78 people went to the movie theater. On Sunday 20 **more** people went to the movie theater than on Saturday. How many people went to the movie theater on Sunday?

Underline the information in orange.

Underline the question in blue.

Operation:

T	O

Answer: ______________________________

Check your answer: ☐ ☐ ☐ = ☐

Compound Word Problems

Let's Connect

- What information is needed to calculate how many containers  has collected? Color.

  ◯  has collected 20 containers.

  ◯  has collected 30 jars and 25 bottles.

  ◯  has collected 20 more containers than .

Word Focus

In math, **compound** means many parts.

- To calculate the number of containers collected by , what calculations will you make? Show your work.

Let's Learn

Compound word problems involve more than one operation.

 collected 30  and 25 . If  collected 20 more containers than , how many containers did  collect?

To solve this word problem, consider:

Information	 : 30  and 25   : 20 **more** containers than .
Question	How many containers did  collect?

Read the problem carefully to find the information needed to answer the question. Then do the pre-calculations.

Pre-Calculations

Information Needed	Total number of containers collected by .
Information Given	30  and 25 
Operation	$30 + 25 = 55$

Now you have the necessary information to answer the question.

Write the operation and find the answer.	$55 + 20 = 75$
Write the answer.	 collected 75 containers.

Let's Practice

1. Solve the following problem. Analyze

a. Leanne had 58 marbles. She gives 24 to her friends and loses 14. How many marbles does Leanne have left over?

Underline the information in orange.

Underline the question in blue.

Pre-Calculations

Information Needed ______________________________

____

Information Given ______________________________

____

Operation

Now you have the information you need to answer the question.

Operation

Answer ______________________________

Quiz Yourself

Solve.

- Michelle is reading a book with 59 pages.
  Last Monday she read 10 pages and on Tuesday she read 5 **more** pages than on Monday.
  How many pages does Michelle have left to read?

Answer ____________________

Exam Strategies

Look and Learn

Mark the correct answer with an ✗.

General instructions

Read the word problem and answer <u>questions 1 and 2</u>.

Instructions for a group of questions

Mia and Sean collect pictures of soccer players. Mia has 35 pictures and Sean gives her 10 of his 47 pictures.

The context gives you the information to answer the group of questions.

1 How many pictures does Mia have **now**?

- A 25
- B 35
- ☒ C 45

There are two questions that use the same information.

2 Which **operation** represents the number of pictures Sean has left?

- A 35 – 10
- ☒ B 47 – 10
- C 47 – 35

Each question has 3 **choices**. Mark the correct choice with an ✗.

What Did You Learn?

Final Evaluation

Numbers Up To 100 and the Decimal Numbering System

1. Write the number represented by the blocks. Then decompose the number.

a.

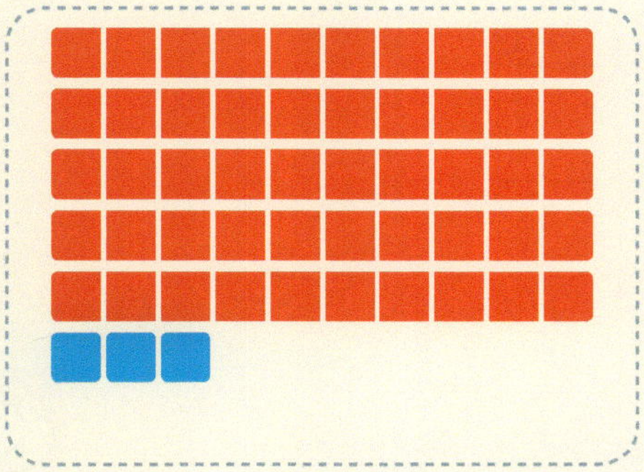

☐ T + ☐ O

☐ + ☐

b.

☐ T + ☐ O

☐ + ☐

Addition and Subtraction

2. Write the operations and solve them.

a. There are 54 apples on one tree and 32 on another. How many apples are there in total?

T	O

b. There are 97 people in a movie theater and 65 leave to buy popcorn. How many people are left in the theater?

T	O

Addition with More than Two Addends

3. Solve.

a. 35 + 20 + 11

[ ] + 11

[ ]

b. 16 + 21 + 42

[ ] + 42

[ ]

Compound Word Problems

4. Solve.

In the first part of a race, Craig ran 30 kilometers. He ran 6 kilometers more in the second part than in the first. How many kilometers did Craig run in all?

Underline the information in [orange marker]. Underline question in [blue marker].

Pre-Calculations

Information Needed ____________________

Information Given ____________________

Operation

Now you have the necessary information to answer the question.

Operation

Answer ____________________

Mark the correct answer with an ✕.

Read and answer questions 5 and 6.

Joe has 45 blocks.
Claudia has 12 more blocks than Joe.
How many blocks does Claudia have?

5. Which operation solves the word problem?

A 45 + 12 =

B 45 − 12 =

C 57 − 12 =

6. What is the answer?

A 33

B 45

C 57

Find Test 4 Study Page

How Did You Do?

For each color a .

Geometry and Measurements

Key Words

length

measure

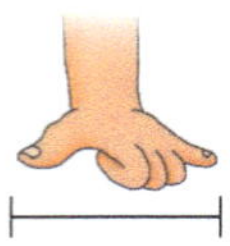

location

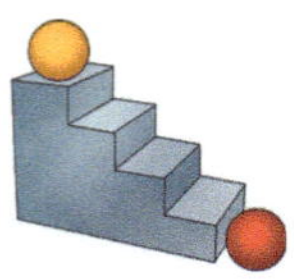

geometric shape

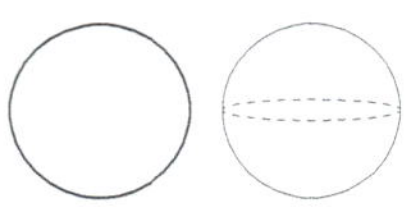

lines

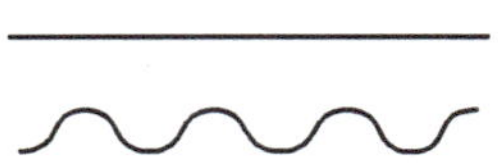

In this unit you will learn to:

- describe the position of objects and people in relation to yourself and others.
- use informal units of measurement for length and time.
- organize events and put them in order.
- recognize lines and two-dimensional geometric shapes.
- do your work in an organized way.

What Do You Know? Initial Evaluation

Look at the picture and answer.

1. Who is on the **bottom floor**? Circle.

2. Where is  ? Color.

   On the top floor.

   On the bottom floor.

3. Who is **in front of** the ticket counter? Circle.

4. Who is **on** the stairs? Circle.

5. Circle the **geometric shapes** you see in the picture.

Section
1 Location

Positions in Relation to Yourself

Let's Connect

- The person in the picture is you and you are looking at the house. Use **Cutout 2** on **page 161** and glue the objects below.

above you	to your **side**	**in front of** you

Let's Learn

The words **left**, **right**, **above**, **below**, **in front of** and **behind** help describe the position of a person, animal or thing in relation to yourself.

For example:

The  is **above** you.

The  is to your **left**.

The  is **in front of** you.

Let's Practice

1. Use **Sticker Set 10** on **page 173**. Stick the objects on the picture. Follow the directions. Understand

a. The  is to your **right**.

b. The  is to your **left**.

c. The  is **in front of** you.

Challenge

As a class, play Simon Says using the position words from the picture. Ready? Simon says, "Stand behind a friend!"

2. Look around your classroom. Do the activities. Recognize

a. Write the names of two classmates or objects that are to your **right**.

- ____________________
- ____________________

b. Draw two objects that are **in front of** you.

c. Write the names of two classmates or objects **behind** you.

- ____________________
- ____________________

d. What is **above** you? Describe.

Above me there is ____________________

____

____

3. Look at the picture. Write **T** for **true** and **F** for **false**. Evaluate

a. ☐  is to your **right**.

b. ☐  is **below** you.

c. ☐  is to your **right**.

d. ☐  is **in front of** you.

Did You Know...?

You can find all kinds of books in a **library**. You should take care of books and return them on the correct date so others can read them as well.

Your Position in Relation to Others

Let's Connect

Go to **Cutout 3** on **page 163**. Glue the pictures.

- Who is **on** the slide?
- Who is **behind** the tree?
- You are . What game is to your **left**?

Let's Learn

- You can describe the **position** of people, animals and objects in relation to other people, animals and objects.

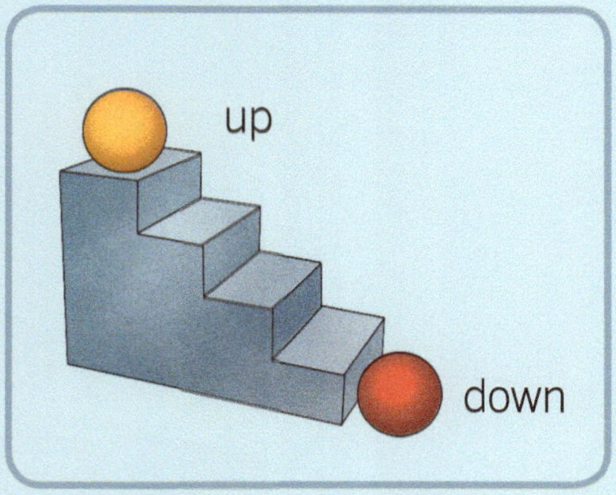

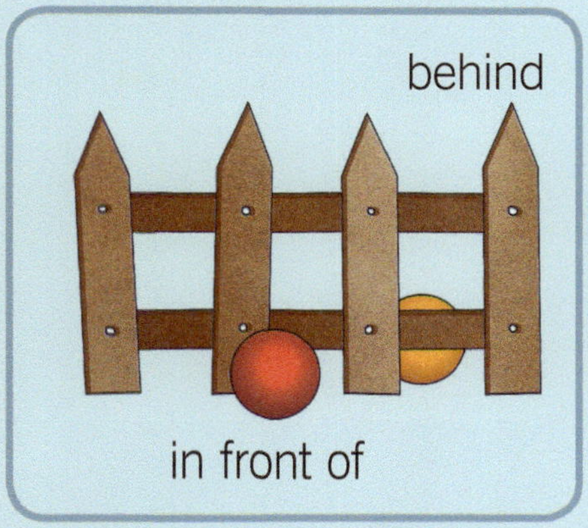

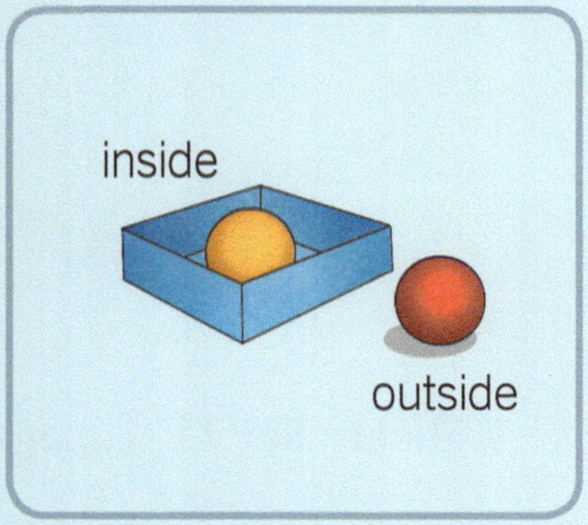

Let's Practice

1. Color the objects in the picture. Recognize

 **under** the 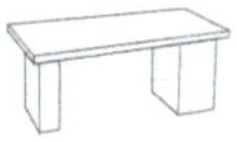

 **on** the 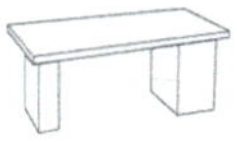

It is important to study and do your homework in a comfortable and **organized** place.

2. Use **Sticker Set 11** on **page 173**. Stick each picture where it belongs. Apply

a. A  on one **side** of the .

b. A  **between** the  and the .

c. A  **on** the .

d. A  **in front of** the .

3. Look at the picture. Circle the **position** that completes the sentence. Understand

a. The  is to the **right** / **left** of .

b. The  is to the **right** / **left** of .

c. The  is **in front of** / **behind** the .

Quiz Yourself

Read the description. Mark Martin's drawing with a ✔.

Martin is **between** his parents. **Behind** them there is a tree. To the **right** of his father there is a cat.

Section 2

Measuring Time and Length

Daily Activities

Let's Connect

- What are the girl and boy doing? Describe.

 She is ______________________________

____

 He is ______________________________

____

- Whose activity takes **more time**? Circle.

Education through Values

When you brush your teeth, do not let the water run. You will save water and help take care of the Earth.

Let's Learn

Daily activities take different **amounts of time**. In other words, their **duration** varies.

class

takes **more time** than

recess

lunch

takes **less time** than

sleep

Word Focus

Duration is how long something lasts. We measure it in seconds, minutes, hours and other units of time.

Let's Practice

1. Compare the **duration** of each activity. Circle. Compare

a. It takes **more time** / **less time** to eat breakfast than to sleep.

b. It takes **more time** / **less time** to go to the beach than to play a game at recess.

c. Singing a song takes **more time** / **less time** than watching a movie.

Breakfast is the most important meal of the day. It gives you energy to concentrate on activities throughout the day.

Putting Daily Activities in Order

Let's Connect

- What does  do first? ______________________
- What does he do **before** breakfast?

____

- What does he do **after** breakfast?

____

Education through Values

It is important to wake up early and get to class on time.
This shows **respect** for you and your classmates' time.

Let's Learn

Daily activities can be put in **order** based on the time they are done.

1st ▶ You put on your pajamas.

2nd ▶ You go to bed.

Before going to bed, you put on your pajamas.
After putting on your pajamas, you go to bed.

Remember, in Unit 2 you learned that **ordinal numbers** are used to put things in order.

Let's Practice

1. Use the pictures from **Cutout 4** on **page 165**. Glue them in the correct order. Order

a. 1st 2nd 3rd

b. 1st 2nd 3rd

Comparing Lengths

Let's Connect

- What object do  and  use to **measure** their notebooks?

____

- Who has the **longer** notebook? Circle.

Let's Learn

To **measure** the **length** of an object, we can use parts of our body or objects as **units of measurement**. These are called **unofficial** units of measurements.

Body Parts

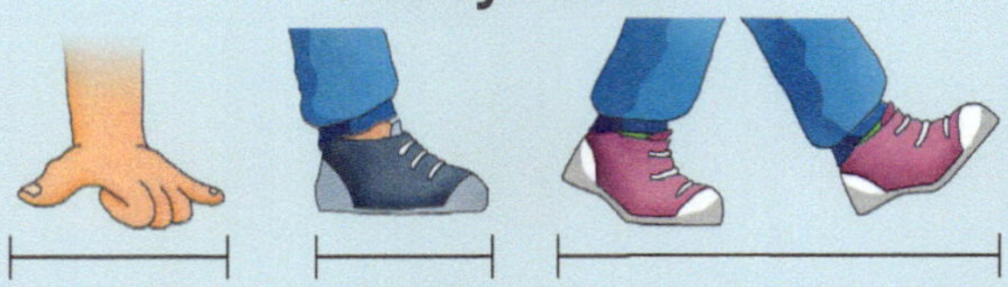

hand | foot | steps

Objects

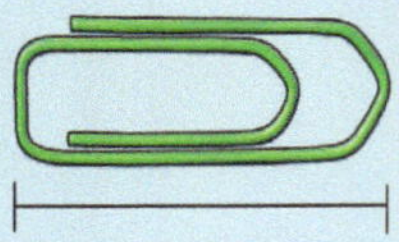

paper clip

Tip
Use **longer** for length and **taller** for height.

The length of an object tells us if it is **longer**, **taller** or **shorter** than another object.

The  measures **6** paper clips.
The  measures **8** paper clips.

The  is **shorter** than the .
The  is **longer** than the .

Let's Practice

1. Circle the **longer** or **taller** object or animal. Recognize

a.

d.

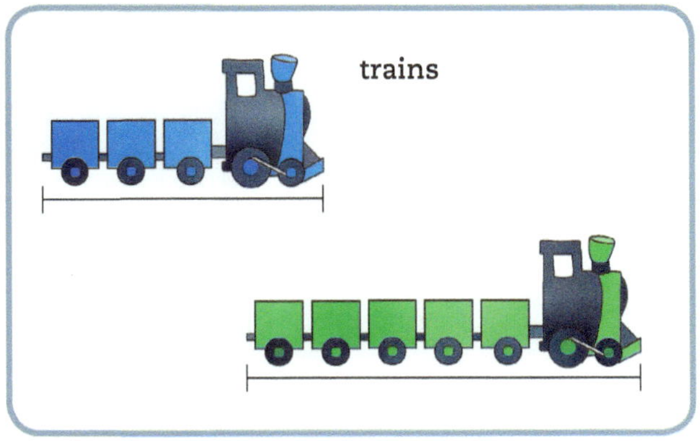

b.

e.

c.

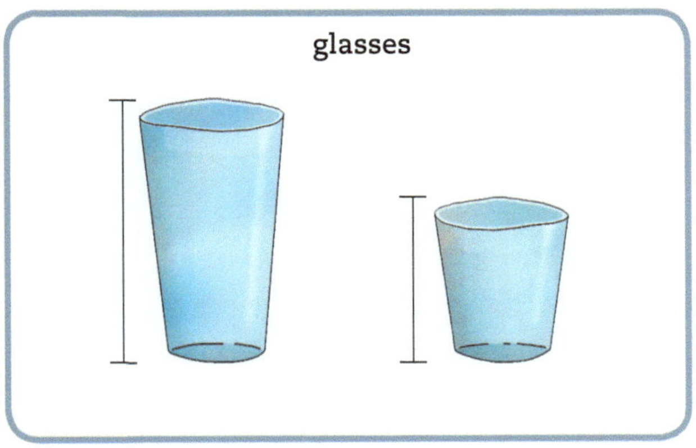

f.

2. Measure the **length** of these objects with the informal units of measurement. Apply

a. The length of the  table is ☐ 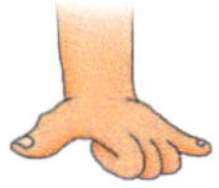 .

b. The length of the  whiteboard is ☐ 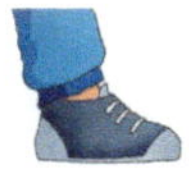 .

c. The length of the 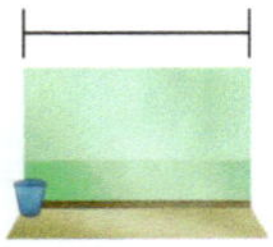 classroom is ☐  .

3. Identify the length of each object in paper clips. Use **Sticker Set 12** on **page 173**. Compare

a. 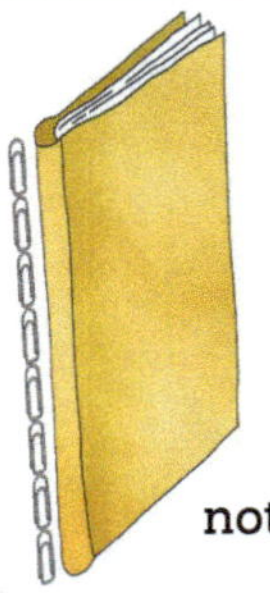 notebook

☐ 

b.  pencil

☐ 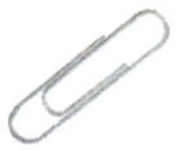

c. 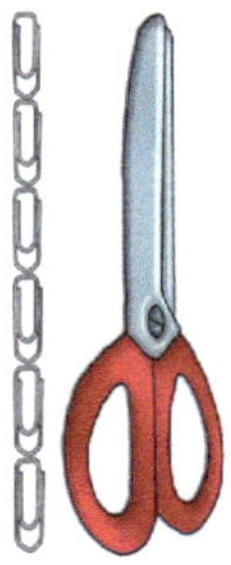 scissors

☐ 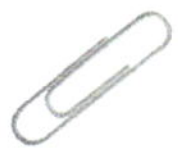

d. Which object is the **longest**?

e. Which object is the **shortest**?

Challenge

Now do the same with your notebook, pencil and scissors. Which object is the longest? Which is the shortest?

Quiz Yourself

Pick a chair with a partner. Use your erasers to measure the chair. Look at the picture and answer.

- What is the chair's measurement?

  Using your eraser:

  ☐ erasers.

  Using your partner's eraser:

  ☐ erasers.

- Did you get the same measurement? Circle.

  yes   no

- Why do you think your measurements are the same as or different from your partner's?

  I think ____________________

  ____

  ____

Tip

You can check your answer by repeating the exercise with your hands.

Education through Values

When you work in pairs, it is important to listen to and respect each other's opinions.

Let's Check!

Positions in Relation to Yourself

1. Look at the picture and answer.

a. Who is to the **right** of Lewis? Circle.

Annie Peter Sofia

b. Who is to the **left** of Lewis and to the **left** of Peter?

____

c. Who is **not** to the **left** of Annie? Circle.

Lewis Peter Sofia

Putting Daily Activities in Order

2. Number the stages of getting dressed from 1st to 3rd.

Duration of Daily Events

3. Color the activity that is true in  .

a. Takes **more time** than brushing your teeth.

Turning on the television.	Blowing out candles.	Playing a soccer game.

b. Takes **less time** than brushing your teeth.

Reading a book with 32 pages.	Closing and opening your eyes.	Eating dinner with your family.

Length of Objects

4. Write the length of each object in paper clips. Circle the **shortest** object.

a.

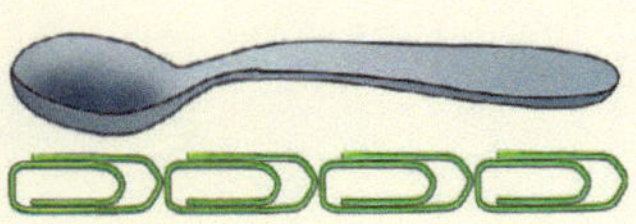

b.

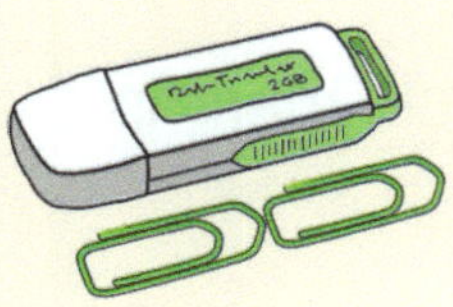

c.

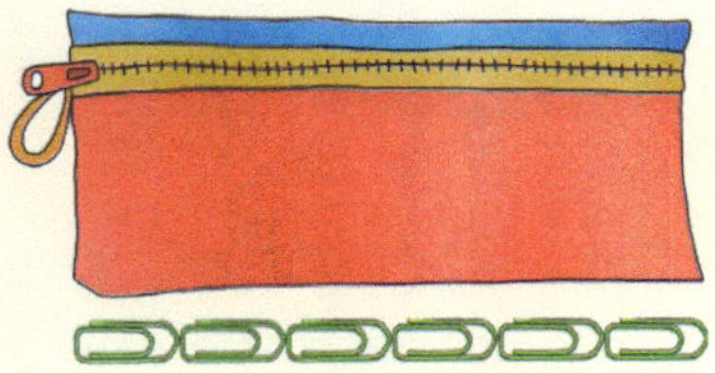

How Did You Do?

For each frog color a lily pad.

Place in Time

Let's Connect

- On which days does  go to school? Circle them in the picture.
- How many days a week does she have guitar lessons? ☐
- On which days of the week does  play soccer?

  ____

- On which days of the week does  have art lessons?

  ____

- If it is Friday, how many days are there until  goes back to school? ☐

Let's Learn

We can use a calendar to locate ourselves in time and put events in order.

- A calendar has 12 **months**.

January	July
February	August
March	September
April	October
May	November
June	December

- Each month is organized into weeks. One **month** has 4 to 5 **weeks** and 28 to 31 **days**.

- A **week** has 7 **days**.

M	T	W	T	F	S	S
Monday	Tuesday	Wednesday	Thursday	Friday	Saturday	Sunday

Did You Know...?

A long time ago, there were only 10 months in our calendar and the year started with March. Different cultures have their own calendars, such as the Mayan calendar, the Hindu calendar and the Jewish calendar.

Let's Practice

1. Name the **month** when each event happens. **Order** them from 1st to 3rd. Apply

a. Christmas is in ______________________________. ◯

b. Valentine's Day is in ______________________________. ◯

c. Mother's Day is in ______________________________. ◯

2. Complete the 1st grade schedule using **Sticker Set 13** on **page 173**. Apply

1st Grade Schedule					
	Monday	**Tuesday**	**Wednesday**	**Thursday**	**Friday**
1 2	Language			Language	Language
3 4		Social Studies		Physical Education (PE)	
5 6	Physical Education (PE)	Language	Social Studies		English

3. Write your birthday. Then write the birthdays of 3 classmates.

a. My birthday is on ______________________________.

b. My friend's birthday is on ______________________________.

c. My friend's birthday is on ______________________________.

d. My friend's birthday is on ______________________________.

4. Write the birthdays in order. Apply

1st ______________________________

2nd ______________________________

3rd ______________________________

4th ______________________________

Quiz Yourself

Look at the birth dates of each child and answer.

- Circle the **youngest** student (the one born **after** everyone else).
- How many days **younger** is  than ? ☐
- How many months **older** is  than ? ☐

Section
4 Lines and Geometric Shapes

Straight and Curved Lines

Let's Connect

line 1

line 2

- If you place a ruler next to each line, which one follows the ruler? Circle.

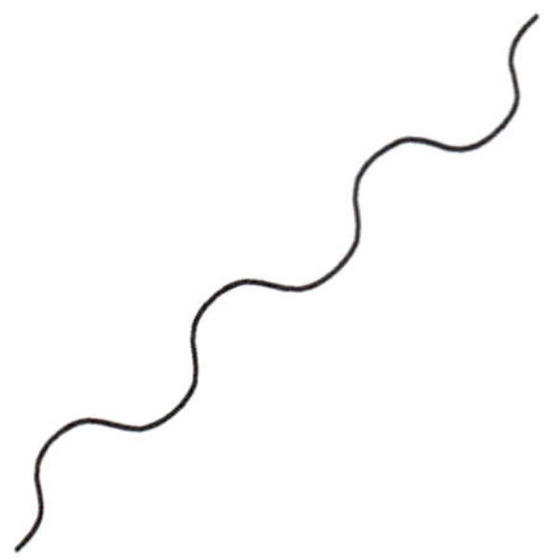

Let's Learn

Lines can be **straight** or **curved**.

straight lines	curved lines
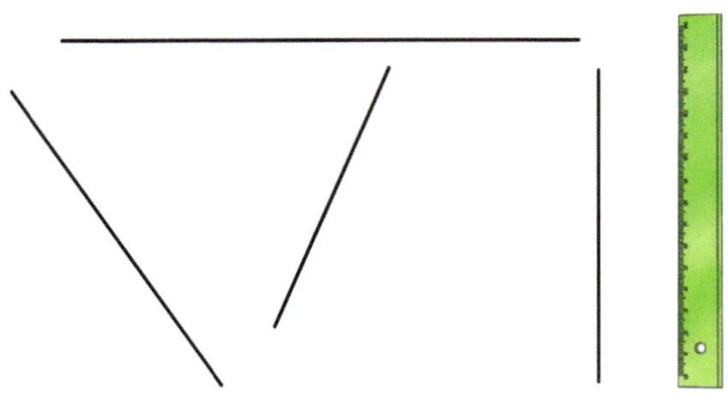	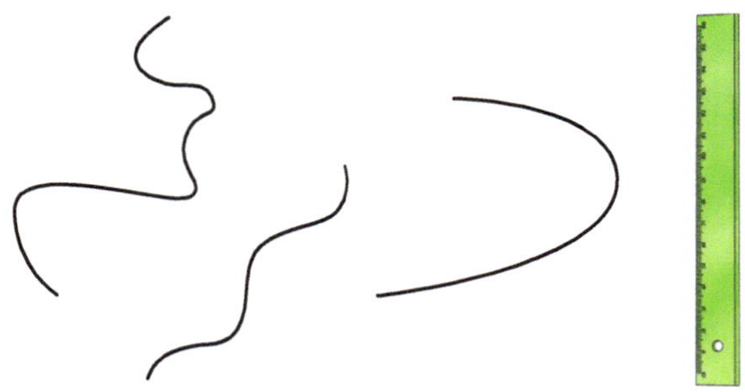
Follow the shape of a ruler.	Do not follow the shape of a ruler.

Let's Practice

1. Circle all the **curved lines**. Identify

2. Draw lines according to the instructions. You can use your ruler. Apply

a. curved lines

b. straight lines

3. Color the letters made by only **straight lines** in . Color the letters made by **curved lines** and **straight lines** in . Identify

a. DUCK

b. ANT

c. CAT

4. Draw a pencil using only **straight lines**. Represent

What shape are the lines of the letters in your name? Look around you: what straight and curved lines do you see in your classroom?

Two-Dimensional Shapes

Let's Connect

- What parts of the train are made up **only** of **curved lines**? Color in .
- What parts of the train are made up **only** of **straight lines**? Color in .
- Which shape does the **smokestack** look like? Circle.

Word Focus

A **smokestack** is a pipe where smoke from a factory, ship or train goes outside.

Let's Learn

Two-dimensional shapes are flat. These can be drawn using straight and curved lines. They are also called **geometric shapes**.

- Two-dimensional shapes with straight lines.

triangle

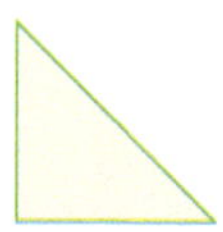

square

rectangle

- Two-dimensional shapes with curved lines.

circle

Let's Practice

1. Match each drawing to the correct geometric shape. Relate

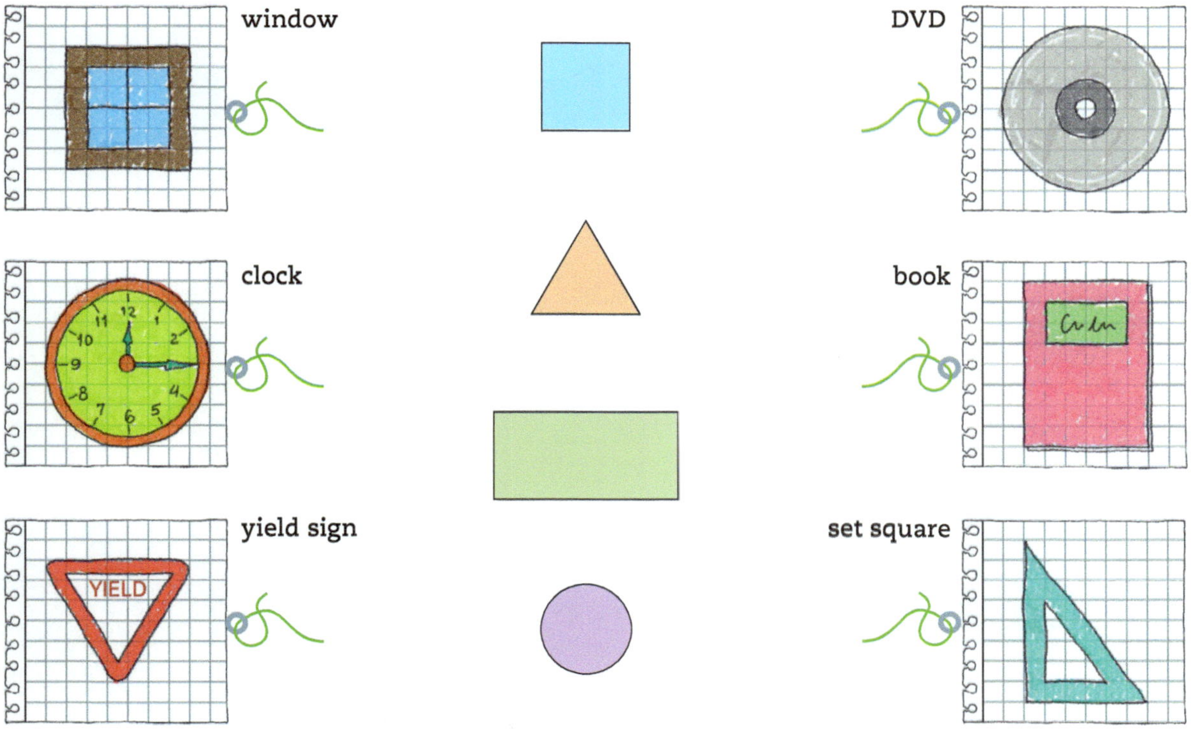

2. Color the geometric shapes. Use the color key. Recognize

- circles
- triangles
- squares

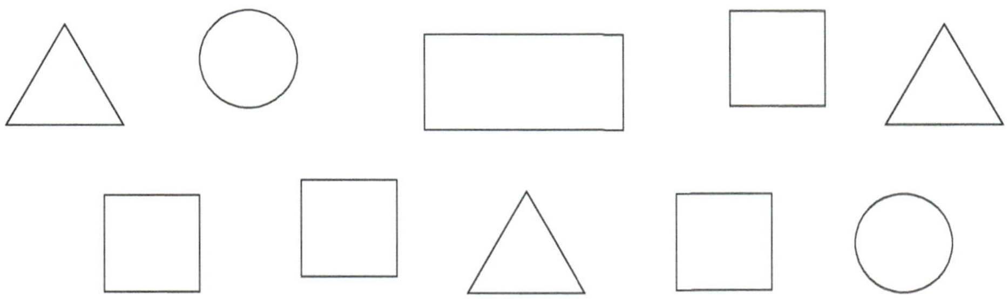

3. Draw and label other everyday objects using the shapes. Apply

Three-Dimensional Shapes

Let's Connect

Use **Cutout 5** on **page 165**. Glue the pictures.

- Which object has the shape of a 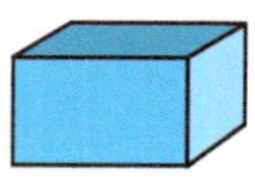 ?
- Which object has the shape of a 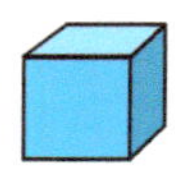 ?
- Which object has the shape of a 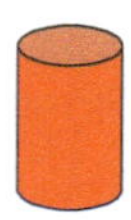 ?

Fun Fact!

Two-dimensional and three-dimensional are often written as 2-D and 3-D. Have you seen these abbreviations before?

Let's Learn

Three-dimensional shapes are **solid figures** that look like real-life objects.

cube	rectangular prism	triangular prism
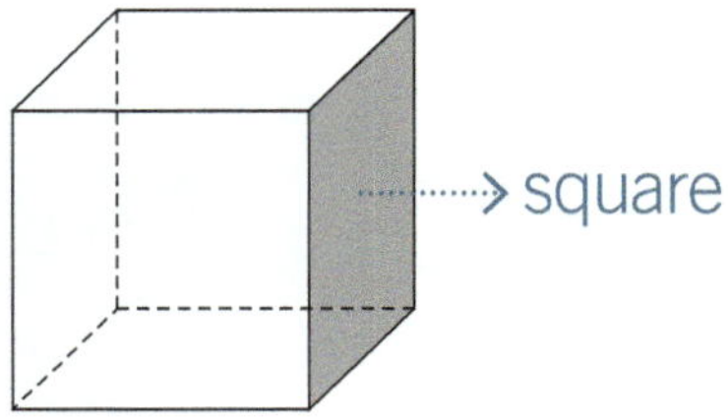	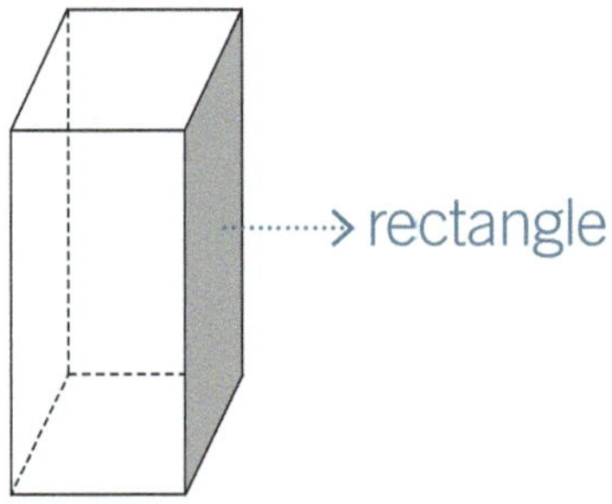	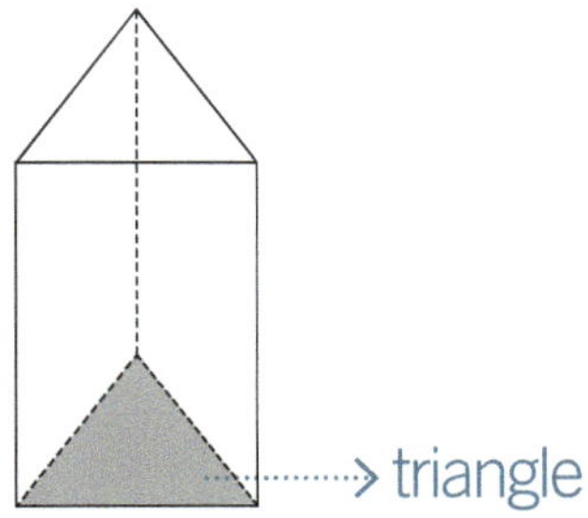

sphere	cone	cylinder
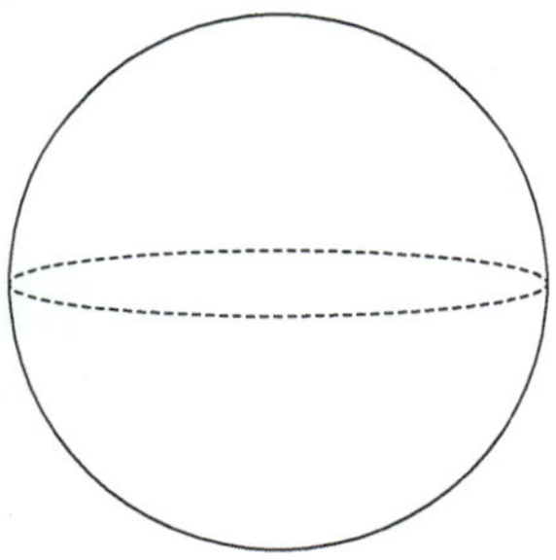	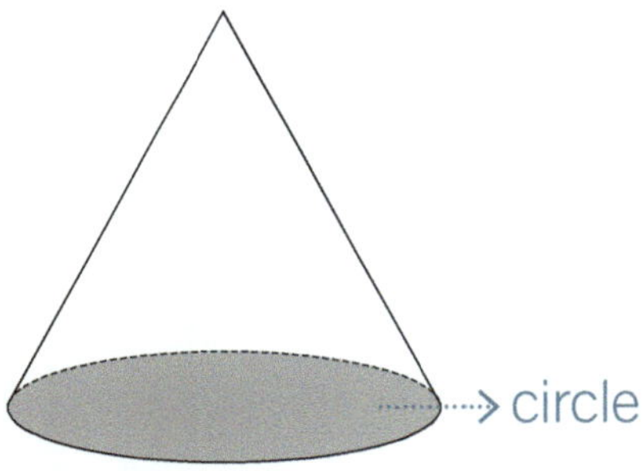	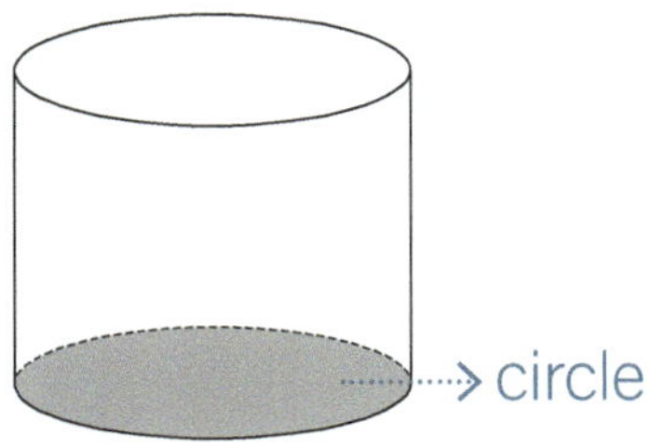

Let's Practice

1. Use **Sticker Set 14** on **page 173**. Put the stickers in the correct box. Relate

a. cube

b. sphere

c. cone

Challenge

With a partner, find an example of each type of three-dimensional shape in the picture on page 144.

1. Match each object to the correct geometric shape. Relate

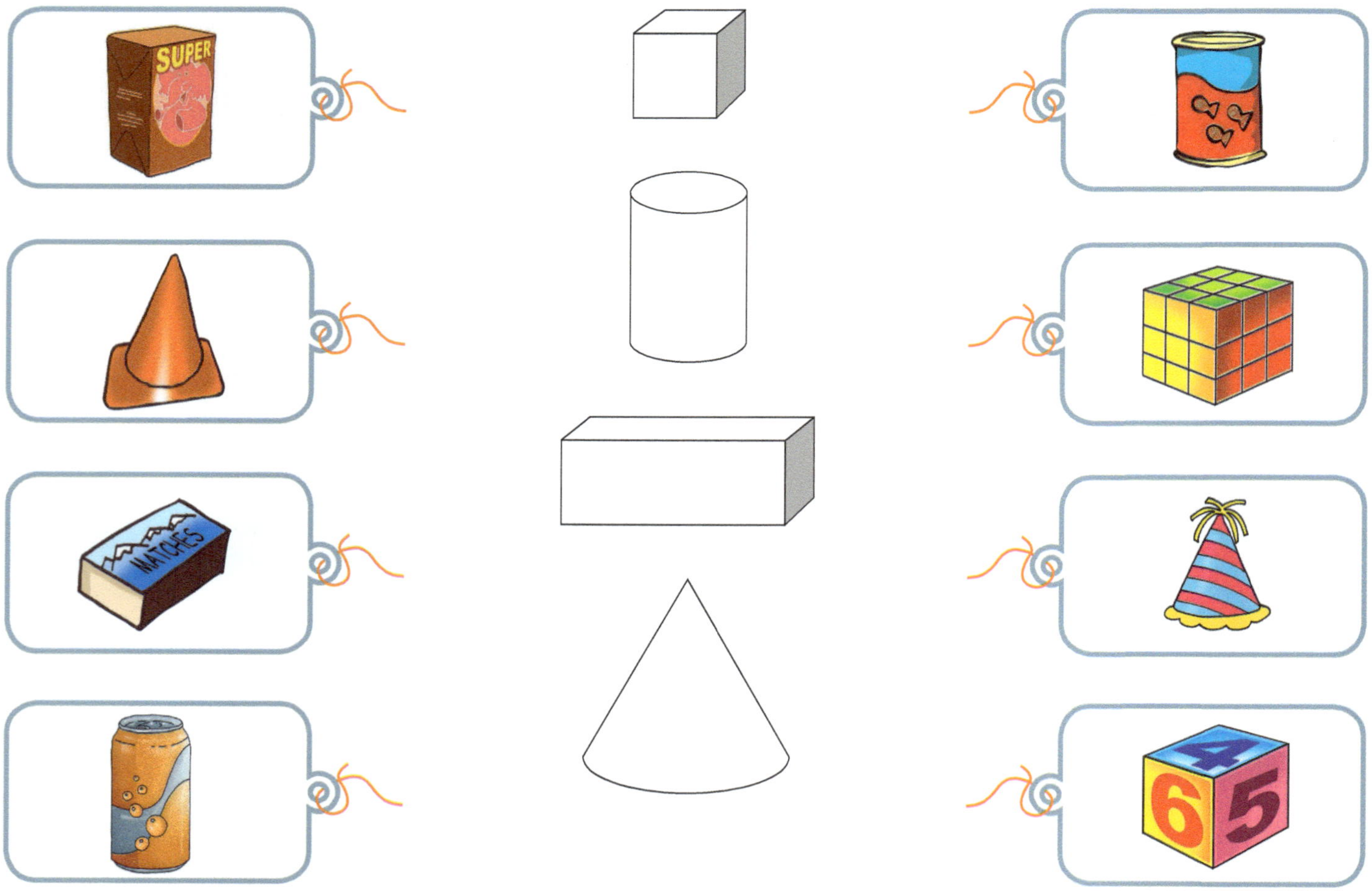

2. Count the shapes. Write the quantity in the boxes. Classify

a. There are ☐ spheres.

b. There are ☐ cylinders.

c. There are ☐ rectangular prisms.

d. There are ☐ triangular prisms.

3. Use **Cutout 6** on **page 167**. Complete. Analyze

cube	rectangular prism	triangular prism
Quantity:	Quantity:	Quantity:
• squares ☐	• rectangles ☐	• rectangles ☐ • triangles ☐

Quiz Yourself

Look at the figures and answer.

- How many **squares** are there?

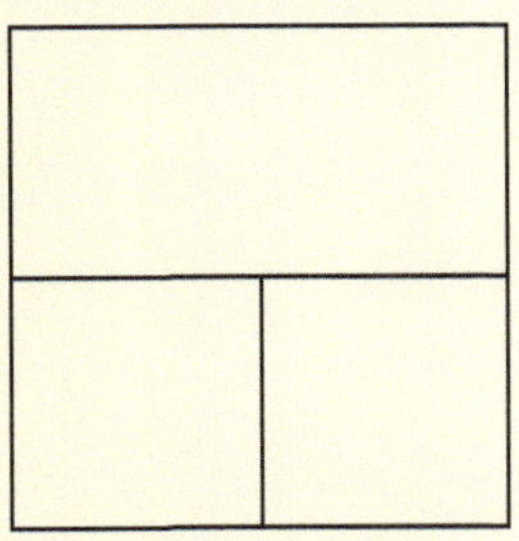

There are ☐ squares.

- How many **triangles** are there?

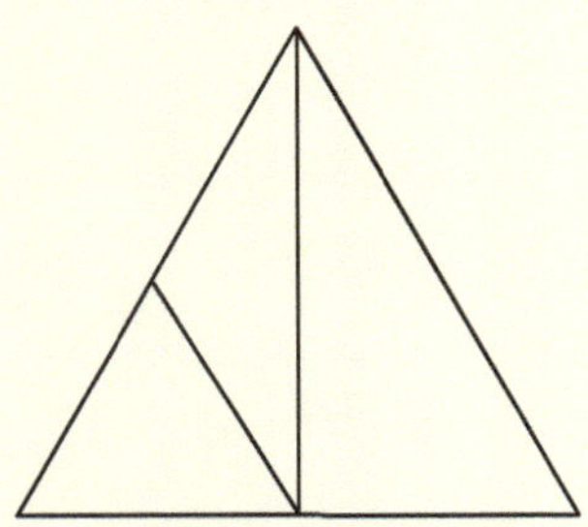

There are ☐ triangles.

Exam Strategies

Look and Learn

Mark the correct answer with an ✗.

Read the instructions.

1 Lucas says a **rectangular prism** is made up of 6 rectangles, and his friend Ian says it is made up of 8 rectangles.

Who is **correct**?

A Ian.

☒ B Lucas.

C Neither.

Read the information carefully. You need to understand this information to answer the question.

Read and understand the question. Find a strategy to answer it.

There are 3 possible answers. Only 1 answer is correct. Mark the correct answer with an ✗. Remember that a rectangular prism is a three-dimensional geometric shape.

Your Turn!

Mark the correct answer with an ✗.

2 Which 3-dimensional shape is made up of only squares?

A Cube.

B Rectangular prism.

C Triangular prism.

What Did You Learn?

Final Evaluation

Location

1. Circle the girl to the right of [girl icon] in [blue]. Circle the girl to her left in [red].

Measuring Length

2. Measure the length of the objects using a paper clip.

a. My  measures ☐ paper clips.

b. My  measures ☐ paper clips.

c. My 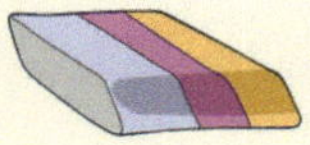 measures ☐ paper clips.

Place in Time

3. Match the ordinal numbers with the dates in the order of their occurrence.

1st	International Labor Day May 1st
2nd	Columbus Day October 12th
3rd	International Women's Day March 8th

Straight and Curved Lines

4. Color the flower drawn with only straight lines in blue.
Color the flower drawn with only curved lines in red.

Two-Dimensional Geometric Shapes

5. Match each shape with its name.

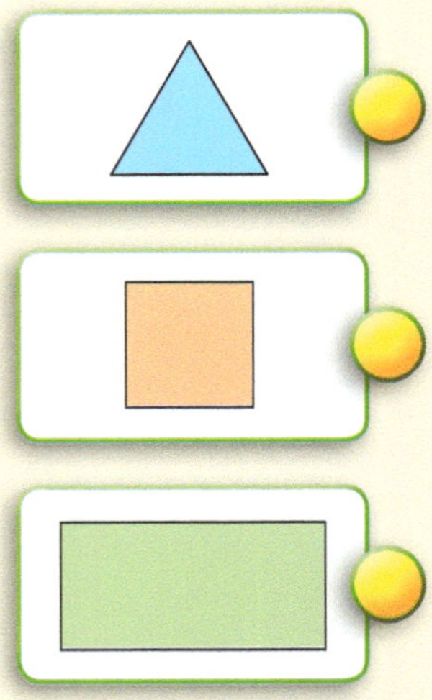

- square
- rectangle
- circle
- triangle

Three-Dimensional Geometric Shapes

6. Look at the three-dimensional shapes and write the quantities.

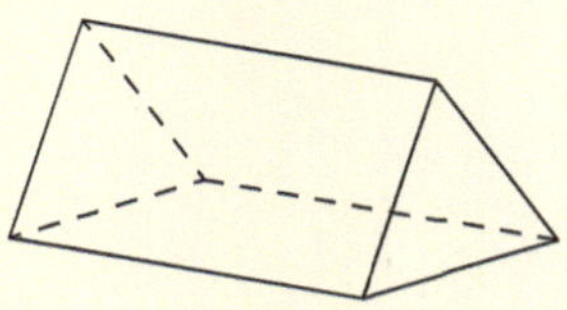

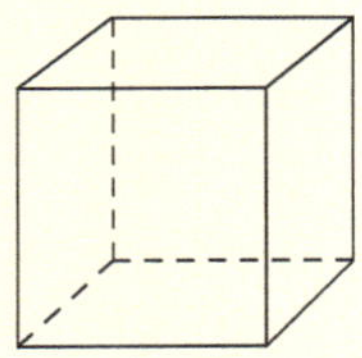

A ☐ triangles ☐ rectangles

B ☐ squares

Mark the correct answer with an ✕.

7. Which drawing looks like a **circle**?

A 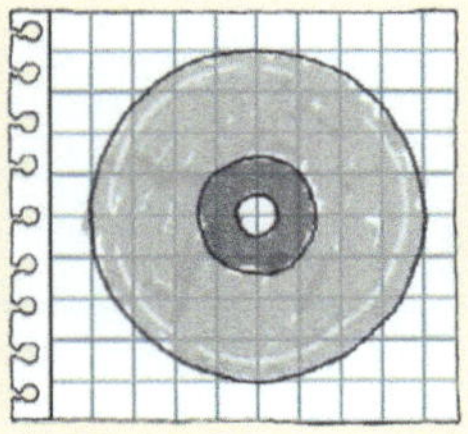

B 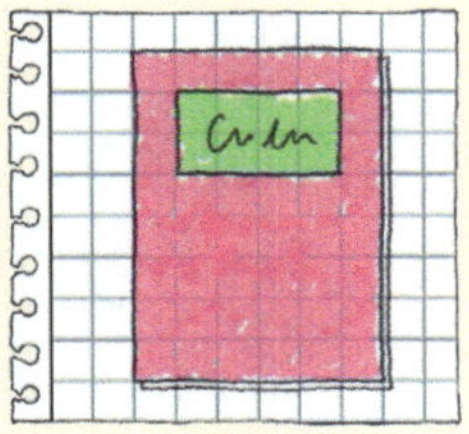

C 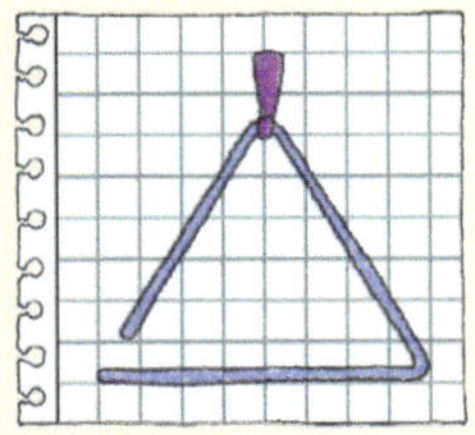

8. Which object looks like a **cone**?

A 

B 

C 

9. How many squares are there in the figure?

There are ☐ squares.

Find Test 5 Study Page

How Did You Do?

For each 🐸 color a ⬭.

Glossary

1.1 Key Words Unit 1

add – *v*, to combine two or more numbers

combine – *v*, to join or put together

count – *v*, to name numbers in order; to determine the total number of something

order – *v*, to arrange or organize something in a methodical way

subtract – *v*, to take away or remove

1.2 Key Words Unit 2

cardinal numbers – *n*, numbers that show a quantity

nominal numbers – *n*, numbers used to identify people or objects

ordinal numbers – *n*, numbers that show a place or position

represent – *v*, to show with symbols or drawings

1.3 Key Words Unit 3

between – *prep*, in the interval separating two numbers; in the space that separates two or more things

change – *v*, to become different

numbered tape – *n*, a strip of paper or cloth used to determine width, length or height

opposite – *adj*, contrary to or totally different from

1.4 Key Words Unit 4

predecessor – *n*, the number that comes directly before another number

successor – *n*, the number that comes directly after another number

1.5 Key Words Unit 5

geometric shape – *n*, a figure that has two or three dimensions

length – *n*, how long something is; the distance from one end to the other

line – *n*, a long, narrow mark between two points

location – *n*, place or position

measure – *v*, to use standard units to discover size or quantity (e.g., length, height, mass, weight, temperature or time)

rotate – *v*, to turn in a circle

A

above – *adj*, in a higher place

addend – *n*, any of the numbers in an addition operation

addition – *n*, the act of combining two or more numbers to find their total

after – *prep*, subsequent in time

around – *adj*, located on every side of

B

backward – *adv*, to or toward the back; to or toward a lesser number

before – *prep*, previous in time

behind – *adj*, at or on the far side of something

below – *adj*, in a lower place

bottom – *n*, the lowest point or part

C

calendar – *n*, a chart that shows the days, weeks and months in a year

collect – *v*, to bring together or gather in one place

column – *n*, a vertical group of information in a chart or graph

30	31	32	33	34	35	36	37	38	39
40	41	42	43	44	45	46	47	48	49
50	51	52	53	54	55	56	57	58	59

compare – *v*, to notice similarities and differences between two or more things

comparison – *n*, an examination of two or more things to find similarities and differences

cone – *n*, a solid with a pointed top with sides that form a circle at the bottom

context – *n*, the surrounding words or facts that help establish meaning

cross out – *v*, to draw a line through something

cube – *n*, a solid that has six square sides

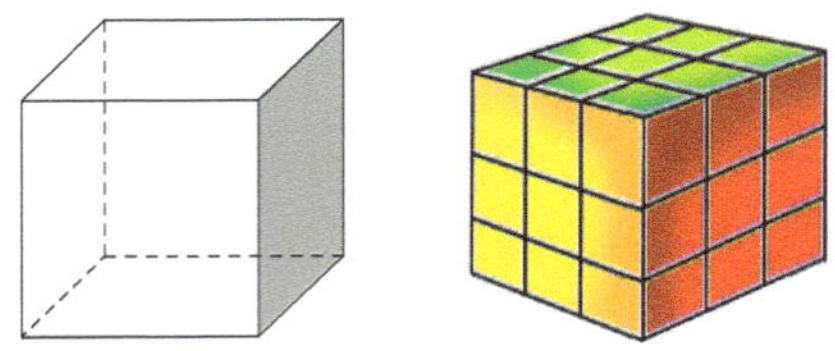

curved – *adj*, not straight; having bumps, bends and irregularities

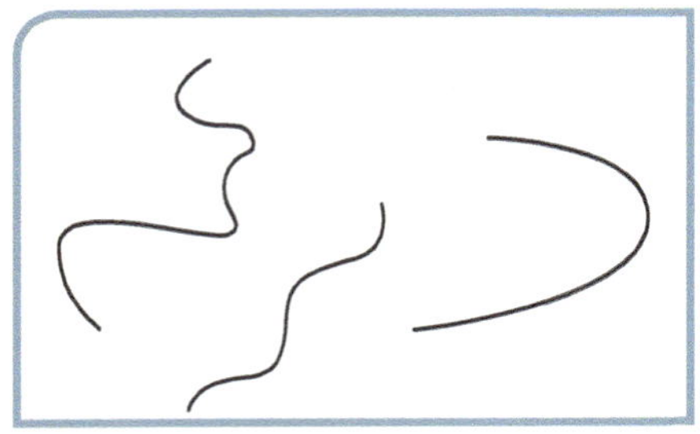

cylinder – *n*, a solid that has a circle at either end

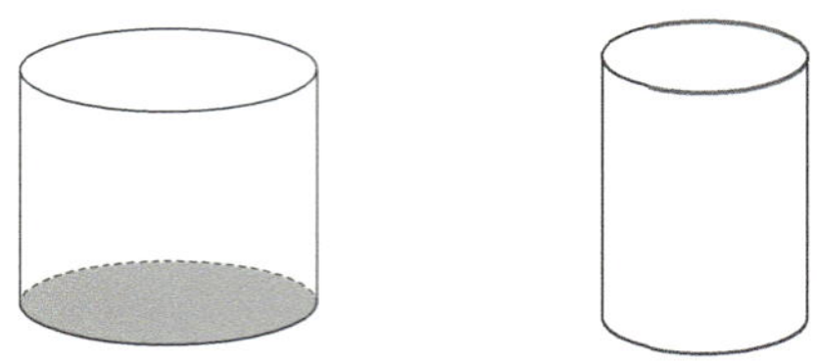

D

day – *n*, a period of time with a duration of 24 hours

M	T	W	T	F	S	S
Monday	Tuesday	Wednesday	Thursday	Friday	Saturday	Sunday

decompose – *v*, to break down into parts

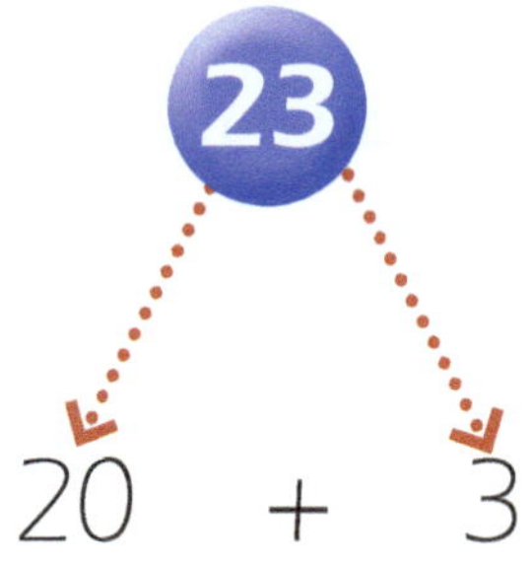

digit – *n*, any of the ten numerals used to indicate numbers

duration – *n*, length of time

E

equal – *v*, to be the same as

equals sign – *n*, a symbol that comes before the result of a math operation like addition or subtraction

even – *adj*, able to be divided by 2; ending in 0, 2, 4, 6 or 8

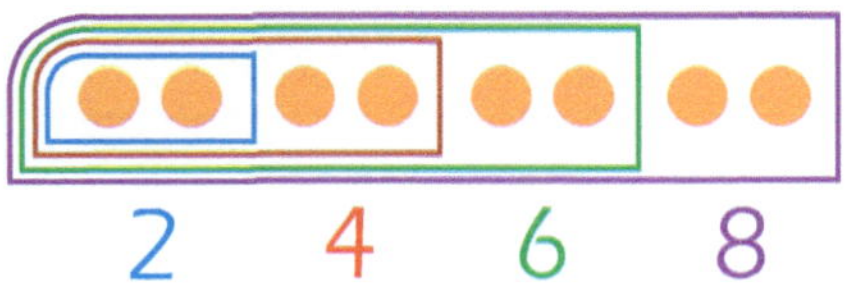

F

fewer – *adj*, a lower number of

floor – *n*, a level of a building

forward – *adv*, to or toward the front; to or toward a greater number

front – *n*, the forward part of something

function – *n*, the purpose or use of something

G

greater – *adj*, more or bigger

greatest – *adj*, the most; the biggest

guess – *v*, to give an approximate answer when you do not have enough information to be exact

I

identify – *v*, to establish what something is

inside – *n*, in the interior of something

L

least – *adv*, smallest in amount

left – *adj*, the west side of something when it faces north; opposite of right

less – *adv*, not as much; fewer

M

minus – *prep*, with the subtraction of

minus sign – *n*, a symbol indicating subtraction

month – *n*, a measure of time based on the movement of the moon that is usually around 4 weeks or 30 days

SEPTEMBER						
M	T	W	T	F	S	S
						1
2	3	4	5	6	7	8
9	10	11	12	13	14	15
16	17	18	19	20	21	22
23	24	25	26	27	28	29
30						

O

odd – *adj*, unable to be divided by 2; ending in 1, 3, 5, 7 or 9

1, 3, 5, 7, 9, 11, ...

offspring – *n*, the young or babies of animals

operation – *n*, a process, such as addition or subtraction, by which numbers interact

$+ \quad - \quad \times \quad \div$

outside – *adj*, on or near the exterior of something; not inside

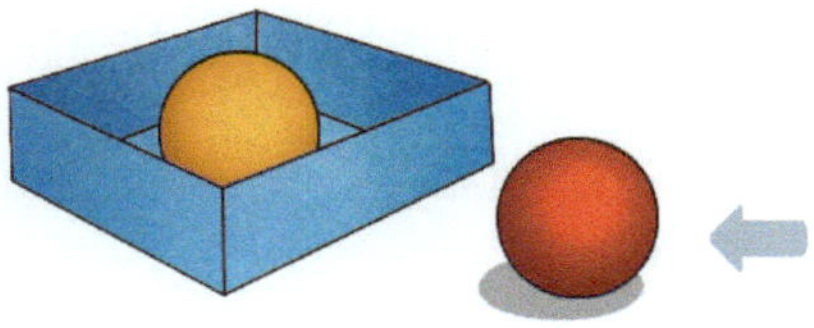

P

place value – *n*, the value of a digit due to its position in a number

T	O
2	3

plus – *prep*, with the addition of

plus sign – *n*, a symbol indicating addition

prove – *v*, to show something is true

Q

quantify – *v*, to express or measure the quantity of

quantity – *n*, the amount or number of something

R

rectangular prism – *n*, a solid that has six rectangular sides

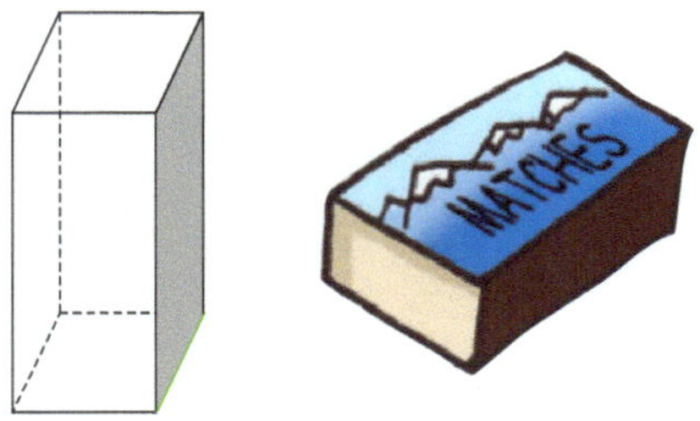

remove – *v*, to take away

right – *adj*, the east side of something when it faces north; opposite of left

row – *n*, a horizontal group of information in a chart

30	31	32	33	34	35	36	37	38	39
40	41	42	43	44	45	46	47	48	49
50	51	52	53	54	55	56	57	58	59

S

schedule – *n*, a table with events and times

side – *n*, a position to the left or right of an object

solve – *v*, to find the solution to a problem

sphere – *n*, a solid that looks like a ball

straight – *adj*, extending in one direction, only without curves

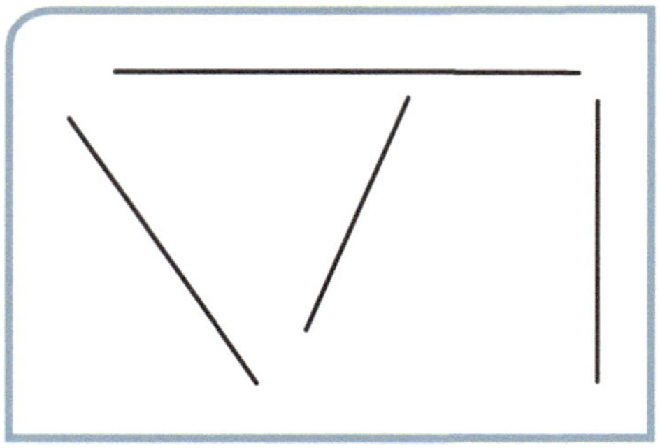

strategy – *n*, a carefully planned way of doing something

system – *n*, a group of things that work together

T

take away – *v*, to remove or subtract

time – *n*, the shift from the past to present to future; the interval between two events; how long something lasts

token – *n*, a small disk or place marker used in a game

top – *n*, the highest point or part

W

week – *n*, a period of seven days

Cutout 1

Use on page 25 (**Unit 1**).

Cutout 2

Use on page 118 (**Unit 5**).

above you

next to you

in front of you

Cutout 3

Use on page 122 (**Unit 5**).

above

behind

left

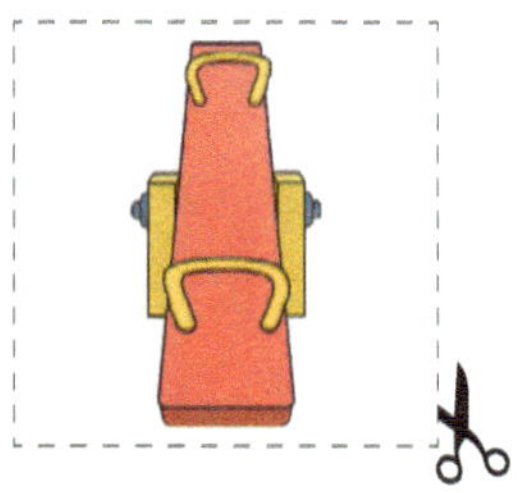

Cutouts

Cutout 4

Use on page 129 (**Unit 5**).

a.

b.

Cutout 5

Use on page 144 (**Unit 5**).

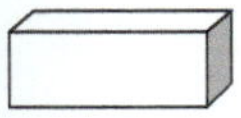

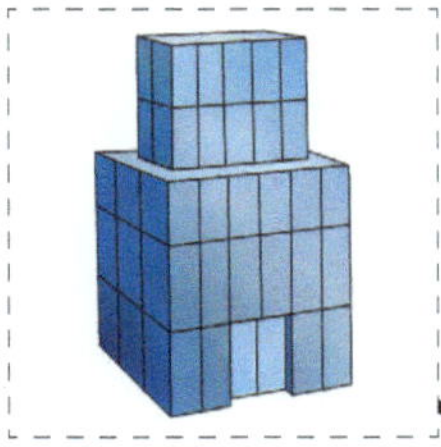
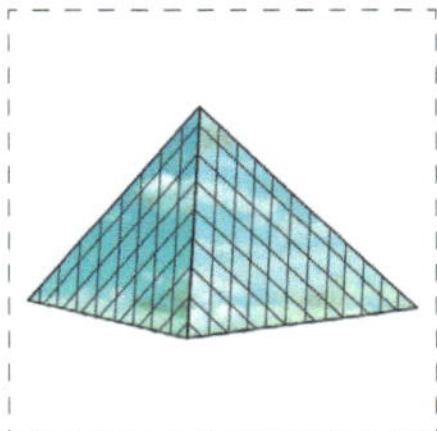

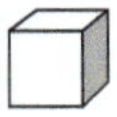

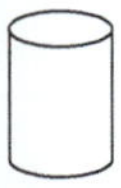
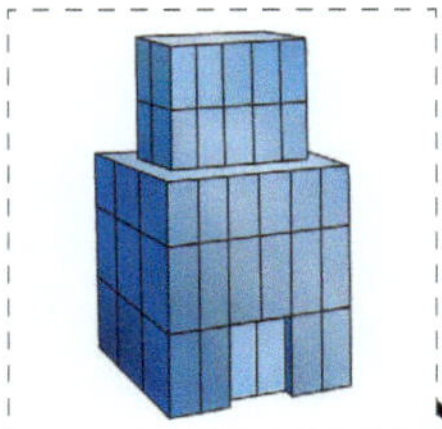
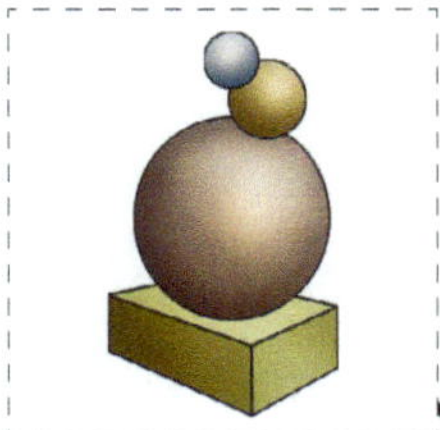
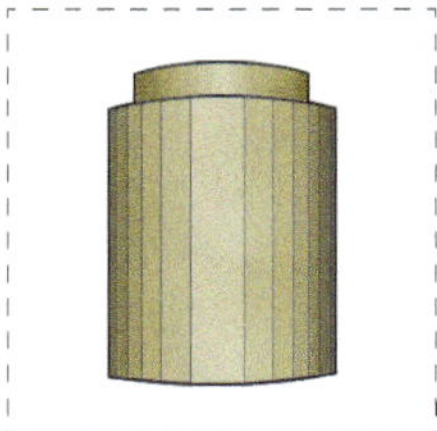

Cutout 6

Use on page 147 (**Unit 5**).

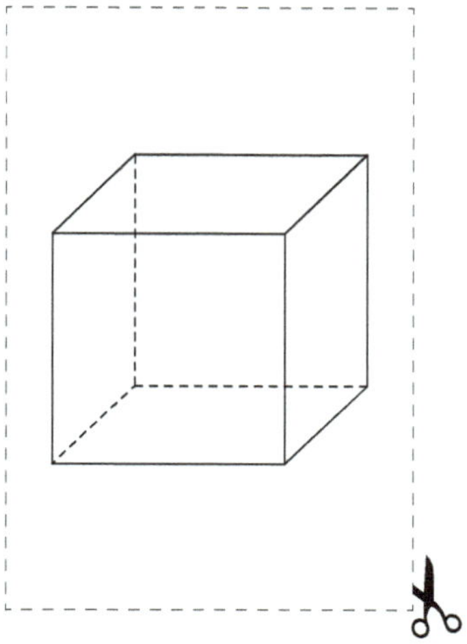

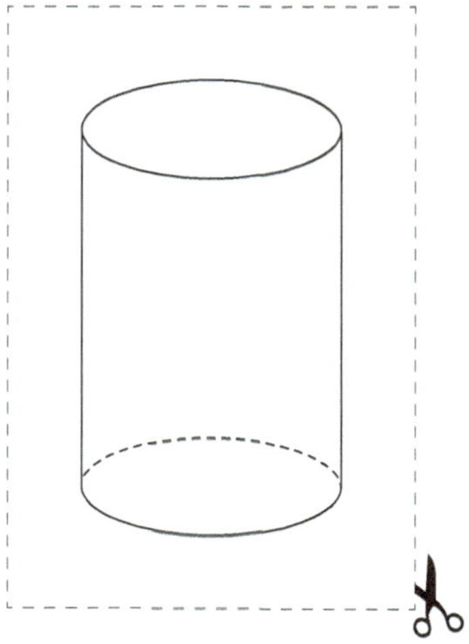

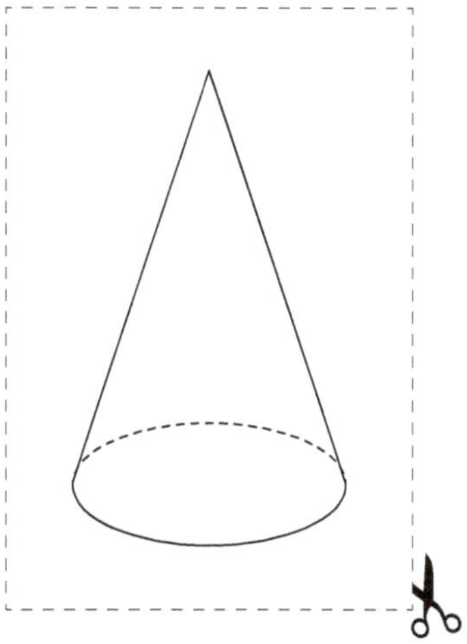

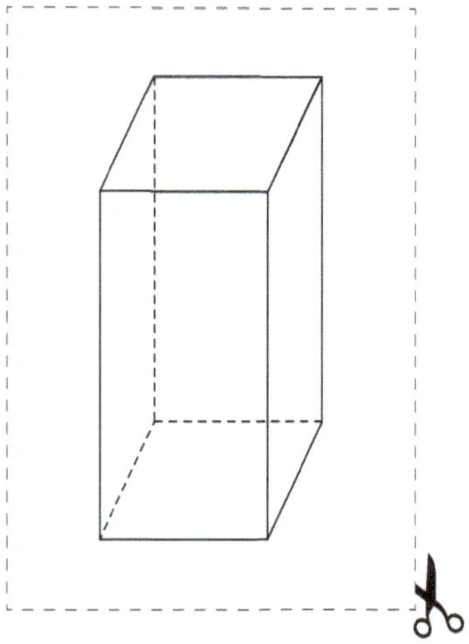

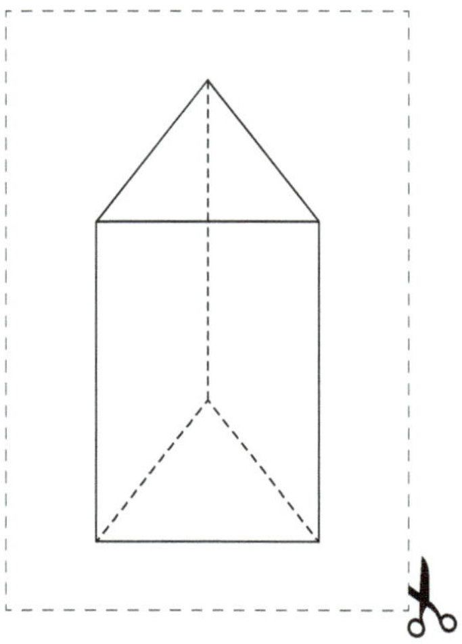

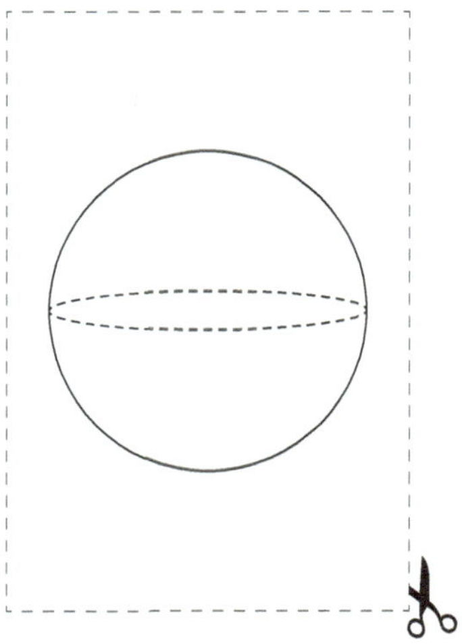

Sticker Set 1

Use on page 9 (**Unit 1**).

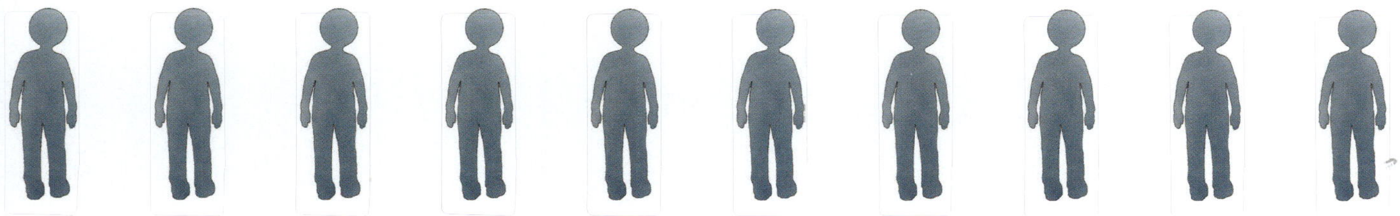

Sticker Set 2

Use on page 34 (**Unit 2**).

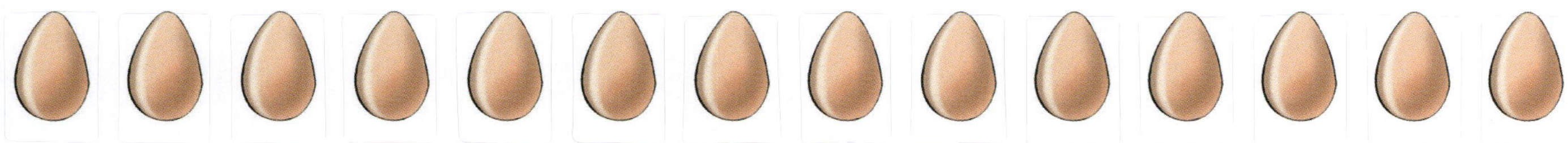

Sticker Set 3

Use on page 37 (**Unit 2**).

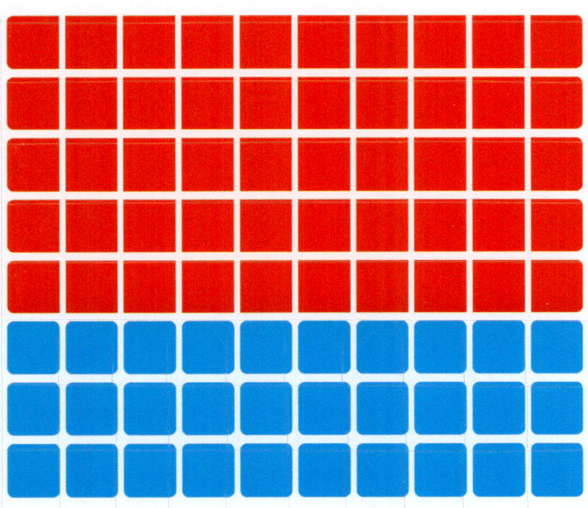

Sticker Set 4

Use on page 40 (**Unit 2**).

Sticker Set 5

Use on page 41 (**Unit 2**).

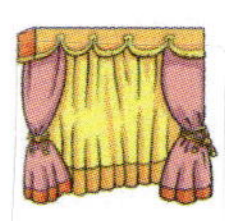

Stickers

Sticker Set 6
Use on page 48
(**Unit 2**).

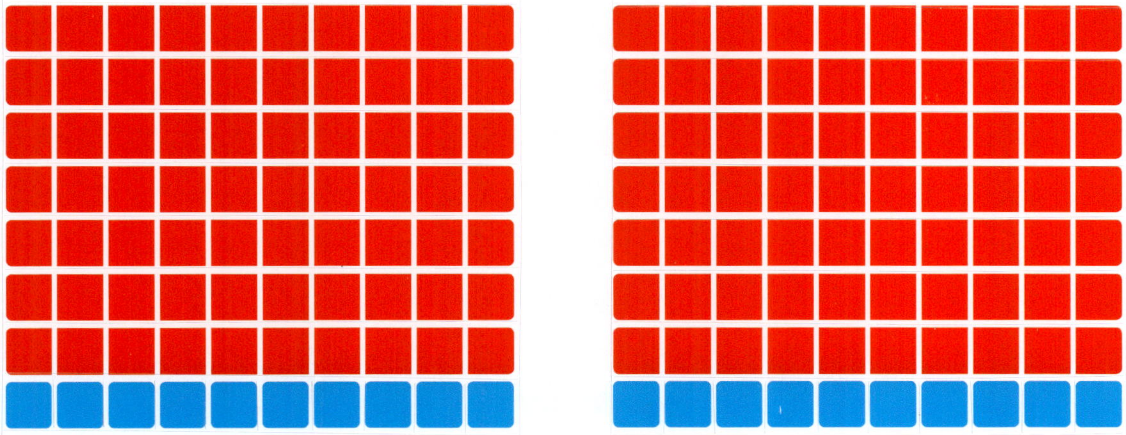

Sticker Set 7
Use on page 53 (**Unit 2**).

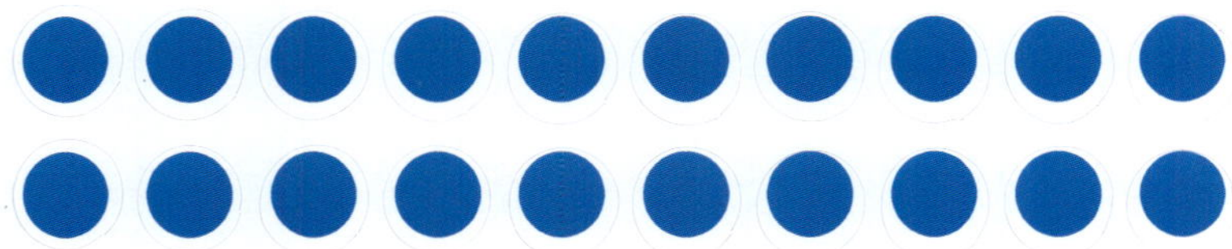

Sticker Set 8
Use on page 98 (**Unit 4**).

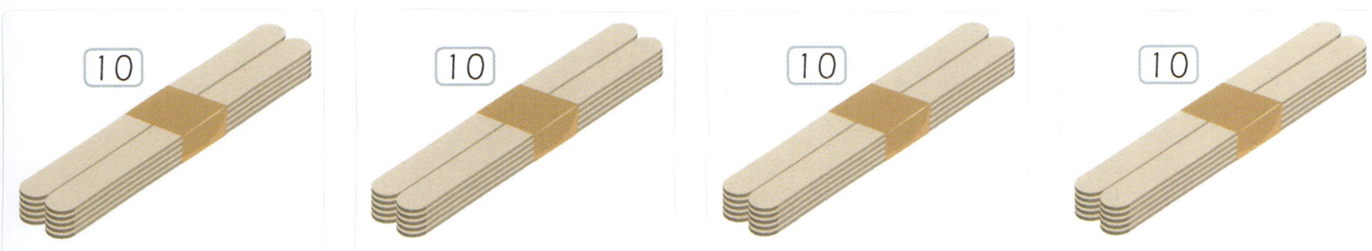

Sticker Set 9
Use on page 101 (**Unit 4**).

Stickers

Sticker Set 10

Use on page 119 (**Unit 5**).

Sticker Set 11

Use on page 124 (**Unit 5**).

Sticker Set 12

Use on page 132 (**Unit 5**).

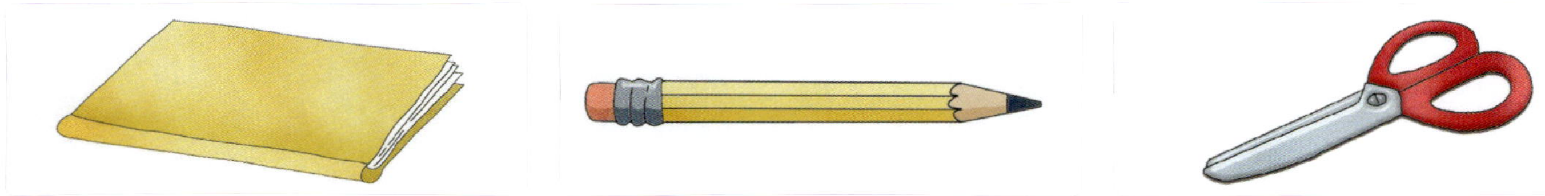

Sticker Set 13

Use on page 138 (**Unit 5**).

Art | Art | Science | Math | Math | Math

Sticker Set 14

Use on page 145 (**Unit 5**).

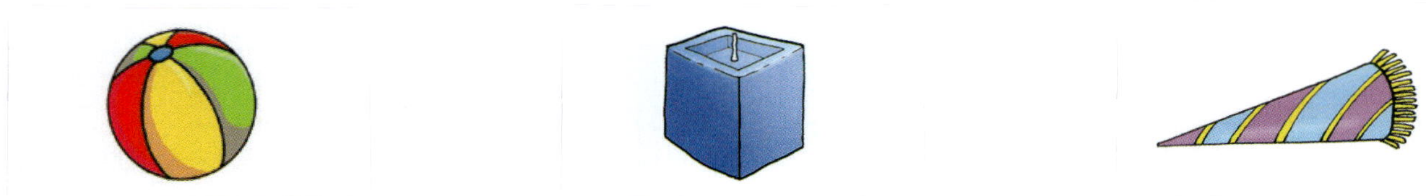

Number Cards

1 0
2 0
3 0

Pathway to Math © Richmond Publishing, S.A. de C.V., 2016

Number Cards

4 0

5 0

6 0

Pathway to Math © Richmond Publishing, S.A. de C.V., 2016

Number Cards

70
80
90

Pathway to Math © Richmond Publishing, S.A. de C.V., 2016

Number Cards

1	2
3	4
5	6

Pathway to Math © Richmond Publishing, S.A. de C.V., 2016

Number Cards

7

8

9

Pathway to Math © Richmond Publishing, S.A. de C.V., 2016

Tokens to Use for Singapore Method

Pathway to Math © Richmond Publishing, S.A. de C.V., 2016

Place Value Table

T	O

Pathway to Math © Richmond Publishing, S.A. de C.V., 2016

Test 1 Study Page • Summary

Unit 1: Numbers and Operations Up To 9

Pathway to Math © Richmond Publishing, S.A. de C.V., 2016

2. Write the operation that describes each situation.

☐ ☐ ☐ = ☐

☐ ☐ ☐ = ☐

glue here

glue here

glue here

glue here

glue here

Test 1 Study Page • Review

Remove, answer, and glue in your notebook.

Unit 1: Numbers and Operations Up To 9

1. Look at the picture. Answer the questions.

- How many are there? Write the number.

 ☐  ☐ 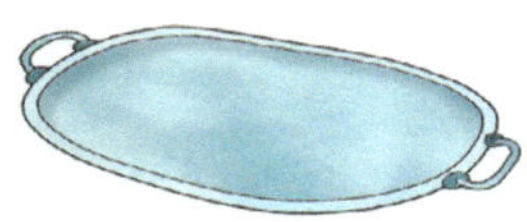 ☐

- Are there **more**  or  ? Circle.

 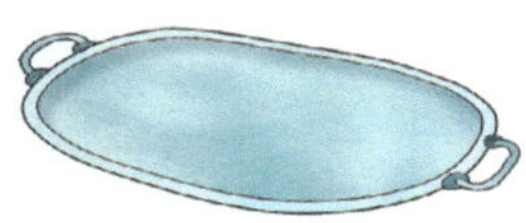

- Is there a birthday hat for **each** boy and girl?

____

Pathway to Math © Richmond Publishing, S.A. de C.V., 2016

Name: ______________________ Grade: __________

Numbers and Operations Up To 9

Represent (Show)	 ● ● 2
Compare and Put in Order	2 is **less than** 3 ● ● ● ● ●
Count	**forward** 1, 2, 3, ... 5, 6, 7, ... **backward** 2, 1, 0 9, 8, 7, ...
Addition	combine – add – move forward $6 + 2 = 8$
Subtraction	take away – remove – move backward $9 - 4 = 5$

Test 2 Study Page • Summary

Unit 2: Numbers Up To 50

2. Complete.

a. In the number 48, the digit 8 represents ☐ ones.

b. In the number 45, the digit 4 represents ☐ ones.

c. In the number 34, the digit 4 represents ☐ ones.

3. **Decompose** each number.

a.

T	O
4	4

▶ ☐ + ☐

b.

T	O
2	1

▶ ☐ + ☐

4. Look for pictures in magazines that use numbers. What kind of numbers are they? Glue and classify the pictures in your notebook.

ordinal | nominal | cardinal

glue here

glue here

glue here

glue here

glue here

Test 2 Study Page • Review

Remove, answer, and glue in your notebook.

Unit 2: Numbers Up To 50

1. Count the cubes by grouping them into tens. Complete.

a.

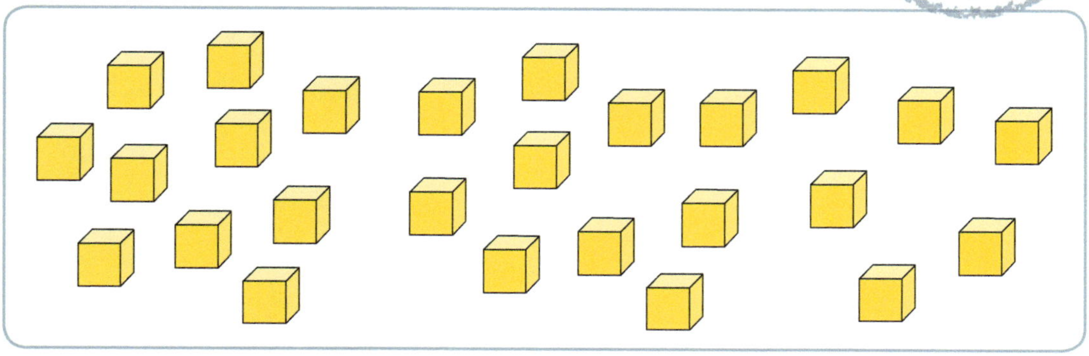

There are ☐ T and ☐ O.

There are ☐ .

b.

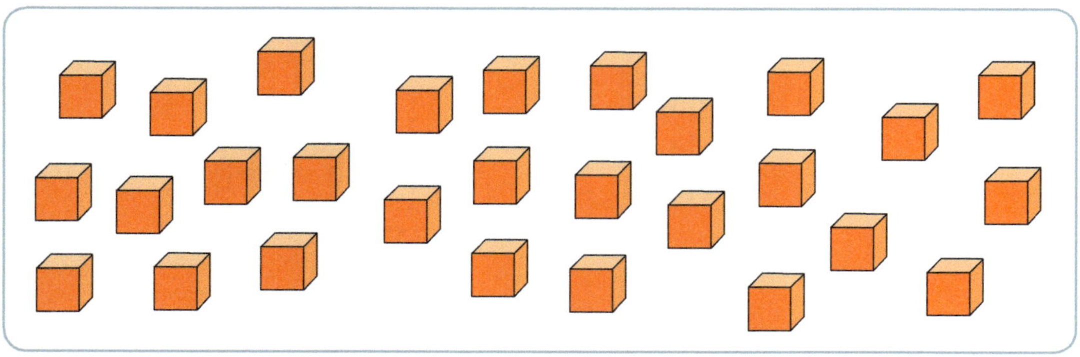

There are ☐ T and ☐ O.

There are ☐ .

Pathway to Math © Richmond Publishing, S.A. de C.V., 2016

Name: ______________________________ Grade: __________

Numbers Up To 50

Represent

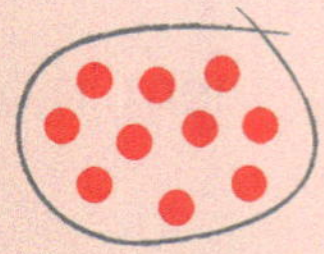 10 

Compare and Put in Order

- from the **least** to the **greatest**

  2 12 22

- from the **greatest** to the **least**

  45 31 25

Count

- one by one 1, 2, 3, 4, 5, 6, ...
- grouping
  - by twos 2, 4, 6, 8, ...
  - by fives 5, 10, 15, 20, ...
  - by tens 10, 20, 30, 40, ...

Composing and Decomposing Numbers

T	O
4	5

40 5 → place value

40 + 5 → grouping

Different Functions of Numbers

ordinal I got 2nd place.

nominal My shirt has the number 14.

cardinal There are 11 players.

Test 3 Study Page • Summary

Unit 3: Operations with Numbers Up To 50

Pathway to Math © Richmond Publishing, S.A. de C.V., 2016

b. There is a bookshelf with 27 books in a classroom.
In the same classroom, there are 11 books on a table.
How many books are in the classroom **in total**?

Underline the **information** in red.

Underline the **question** in blue.

Action: ______________________

Operation: ☐ ☐ ☐ = ☐

Answer: ______________________

Check: ☐ ☐ ☐ = ☐

glue here

glue here

glue here

glue here

glue here

Test 3 Study Page • Review

Remove, answer, and glue in your notebook.

Unit 3: Operations with Numbers Up To 50

1. Solve the problems.

a. There are 24 children on a school bus.
At a bus stop, some children get off and 13 children are left.
How many children got off the bus at the bus stop?

Underline the **information** in orange.

Underline the **question** in blue.

Action: ______________________

Operation: ☐ ☐ ☐ = ☐

Answer: ______________________

Check: ☐ ☐ ☐ = ☐

Pathway to Math © Richmond Publishing, S.A. de C.V., 2016

Name: ______________________________ Grade: __________

Operations with Numbers Up To 50

Written Math Strategies	You can check your answers by applying the relationship between addition and subtraction.
Mental Math Strategies	• Counting.
Word Problems	• Combination word problems. Actions: combine or take away Operations: addition or subtraction • Problems with a change. Actions: add or remove, move forward or backward • Identify the information. • Identify the question. • Write the operation and solve it. • Use the relationship between addition and subtraction to check your answer.

Test 4 Study Page • Summary

Unit 4: Numbers and Operations Up To 100

4. Solve.

The maximum number of points that can be scored in a game is 80. A team scores 76 points in the first round and then loses 56 points in the second round. How many points do they need to reach the maximum score?

Underline the information in orange. Underline the question in blue.

Pre-Calculations

Information Needed ______________________________

Information Given ______________________________

Operation

Now you have the information you need to answer the question.

Operation

Answer ______________________________

Test 4 Study Page • Review

Remove, answer, and glue in your notebook.

Unit 4: Numbers and Operations Up To 100

1. Complete the table with the missing numbers.

80	81			84					
	91					96			

2. Solve.

a. 23 + 7 + 12

☐ + 12

☐

b. 15 + 15 + 18

☐ + 18

☐

3. Decompose the following numbers.

a. 34

☐ T + ☐ O

☐ + ☐

b. 78

☐ T + ☐ O

☐ + ☐

Pathway to Math © Richmond Publishing, S.A. de C.V., 2016

Name: ______________________ Grade: ________

Numbers and Operations Up To 100

Count	0 ➡ 10 ➡ 20 ➡ 30 ➡ 40 ➡ . . .
Predecessor and Successor	predecessor 58 · number 59 · successor 60
Tens and Ones	10 O is equal to 1 T. 50 O is equal to 5 T.
Additive Decomposition	64 · 6 T + 4 O · 60 + 4
Addition and Subtraction	• comparisons • addition with more than 2 addends 25 + 30 + 12
Word Problems	• comparison word problems • compound word problems

Test 5 Study Page • Summary

Unit 5: Geometry and Measurements

3. Circle the **longest** objects.

a.

b.

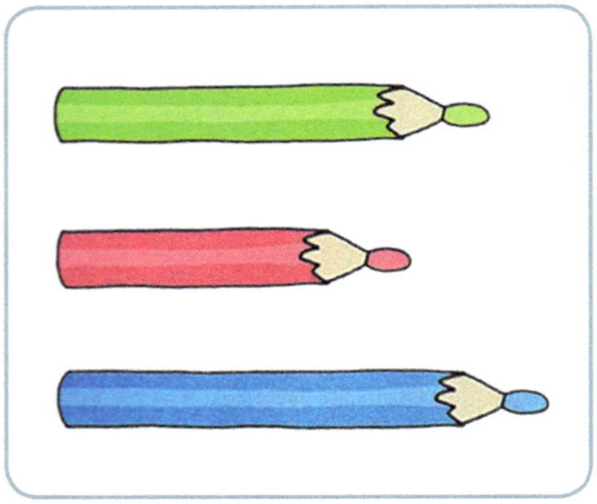

4. Look at a calendar. Put the dates in order.

December 25th
May 21st
September 18th

____
____
____

5. Find pictures of objects in magazines that look like the solid shapes (3-D). Glue them in your notebook.

cylinder

sphere

cube

rectangular prism

glue here
glue here
glue here
glue here
glue here

Test 5 Study Page • Review

Unit 5: Geometry and Measurements

Remove, answer, and glue in your notebook.

1. Color and use the key.

behind the

inside the

to the side of the

in front of the

2. Number the pictures 1st and 2nd.

Name: ______________________________ Grade: __________

Geometry	Location	left/right, above/below, in front of/ behind, inside/outside, between, around
	Straight and Curved Lines	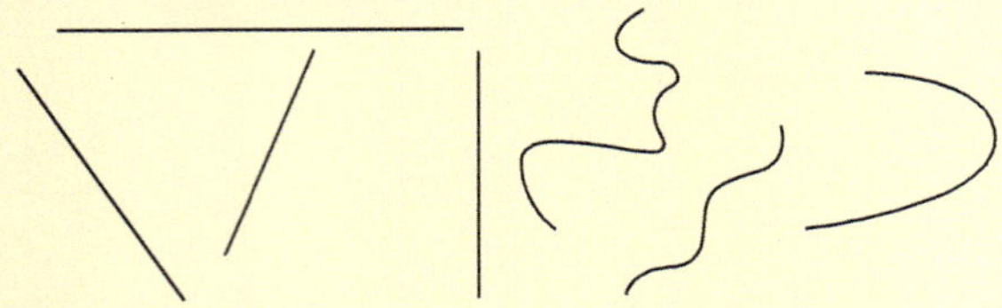
	Two-Dimensional Shapes	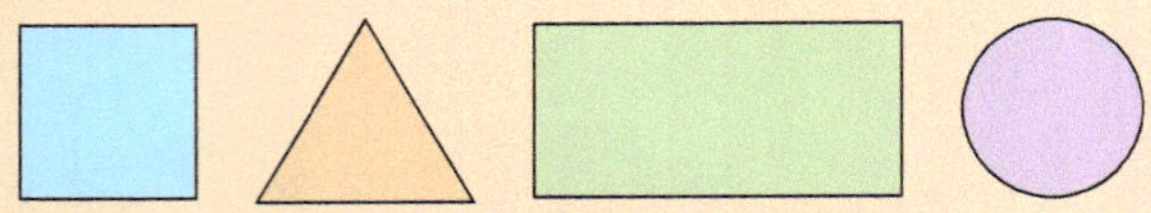
	Three-Dimensional or Solid Shape	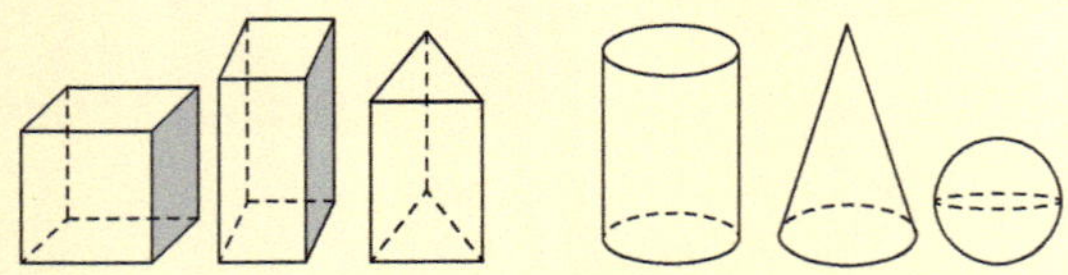
Measurements	Duration of Events	less time · more time
	Putting Events in Order	before · after 1st · 2nd
	Comparing Lengths	 shorter · longer
	Place in Time	months · weeks · days